Cambridge Elements ≡

Elements in Politics and Communication
edited by
Stuart Soroka
University of California, Los Angeles

CONSTRUCTING POLITICAL EXPERTISE IN THE NEWS

Kathleen Searles
Louisiana State University

Yanna Krupnikov
University of Michigan

John Barry Ryan
University of Michigan

Hillary Style
Stony Brook University

CAMBRIDGE
UNIVERSITY PRESS

Shaftesbury Road, Cambridge CB2 8EA, United Kingdom

One Liberty Plaza, 20th Floor, New York, NY 10006, USA

477 Williamstown Road, Port Melbourne, VIC 3207, Australia

314–321, 3rd Floor, Plot 3, Splendor Forum, Jasola District Centre, New Delhi – 110025, India

103 Penang Road, #05–06/07, Visioncrest Commercial, Singapore 238467

Cambridge University Press is part of Cambridge University Press & Assessment, a department of the University of Cambridge.

We share the University's mission to contribute to society through the pursuit of education, learning and research at the highest international levels of excellence.

www.cambridge.org
Information on this title: www.cambridge.org/9781009108430
DOI: 10.1017/9781009104289

© Kathleen Searles, Yanna Krupnikov, John Barry Ryan and Hillary Style 2023

First published 2023

A catalogue record for this publication is available from the British Library.

ISBN 978-1-009-10843-0 Paperback
ISSN 2633-9897 (online)
ISSN 2633-9889 (print)

Constructing Political Expertise in the News

Elements in Politics and Communication

DOI: 10.1017/9781009104289
First published online: January 2023

Kathleen Searles
Louisiana State University

Yanna Krupnikov
University of Michigan

John Barry Ryan
University of Michigan

Hillary Style
Stony Brook University

Author for correspondence: Kathleen Searles, ksearles@lsu.edu

Abstract: Expert news sources in particular offer context and act as translators, communicating complex policy issues to the public. Therefore, expert sources have implications for who, and what, is elevated and legitimized by news coverage. This Element considers patterns in expert sources, focusing on a particular area of expertise: politics. As a starting point, the authors conduct a content analysis to track which types of political experts are most likely to be interviewed and use this analysis to explain patterns in expert sourcing. Building on the source data, there follow experiments and surveys of journalists to consider demand for expert sources. Finally, shifting the analysis to the supply of expert sources, the Element turns to a survey of faculty to track expert experiences with journalists. Jointly, the results suggest that underlying patterns in expert sourcing are a tension between journalists' preferences, the time constraints of producing news, and the preferences of the experts themselves.

Keywords: news, experts, sources, political journalism, political science

ISBNs: 9781009108430 (PB), 9781009104289 (OC)
ISSNs: 2633-9897 (online), 2633-9889 (print)

Contents

1 Pictures of Experts in Our Heads

1.1 Introduction

If the news reflects the pictures in our head, as Lippmann (1922) famously described, then news sources are the main characters. In the event of a car crash, the main characters may include a bystander who offers an eyewitness account, a sheriff who provides additional information about the accident, and a concerned citizen who shares neighborhood frustrations regarding a problematic intersection. Reporting a newsworthy event such as an accident is fairly formulaic: A clear cast of characters, people – who either observed or can comment on the who, what, when, where, and how of a story – contribute to the news narrative (Ross, 2007; Tuchman, 1972).

The task becomes more difficult when the news event is complicated, ambiguous, or unusual. In such cases, reporters often call upon a subset of sources – *expert sources* – to contextualize stories (Diekerhof, 2021; Gans, 1979). A climate researcher, for example, may explain how the weather is affecting local crops, while a scholar of Congress may clarify the history of legislative decision-making. These expert sources fulfill an important function, particularly as newsroom cutbacks mean journalists are increasingly called upon to report on broader geographic and subject areas (Gandy, 1982; Lewis, Williams & Franklin, 2008; Sigel, 1973). With less specialization and fewer resources, journalists are unlikely to have the needed competencies or time to comprehend the scope of a complex story (Coddington & Molyneux, 2021). Such is the case in the domain of politics, where reporting requires background knowledge of political actors, institutions, and policy.

Expert sources can step into this gap, offering (ostensibly) unbiased, factual knowledge to the news article (Albæk, 2011; Shoemaker & Reese, 1996) and adding to perceived journalistic objectivity (Reich, 2011; Steele, 1995). Experts can also lend nuance to a story – sending a signal of in-depth reporting (Boyce, 2006). Inasmuch as journalists see their role as watchdogs, shedding light on politics to hold politicians accountable, expert sources can help ensure reporters get the story right (Galtung, 1995).

The impact of this function goes beyond utility, however; who serves as an expert source affects perceptions not just of the story, but of who gets to be an expert. Expert sources serve as translators of often complex policy issues and ideas to the broader public (Berkowitz & Beach, 1993; Kruvand, 2012; Venger, 2019). When they make it to the news, experts' ideas are elevated, which affects how complicated ideas – often heavily debated and contested by scholars within a given field – come to be defined as conventional wisdom or policy in news coverage (Brown et al., 1987; Merkley, 2020; Tuchman,

1978). Said another way: becoming a news source legitimizes experts. Such legitimization is consequential, as news coverage of politics informs the work of interest groups and lawmakers who look to the news to learn of the problems the public faces (Cook, 2005). With a preference for certainty, these groups are likely to treat these translations as definitional (Esterling, 2009). Thus, the construction of politics by expert sources in the news affects our shared agenda and ultimately, policy (Baumgartner & Jones, 2009; Kingdon, 1984). The result is that both the function and form of an expert source influence the news. In this Element, we consider how expert sources come to be included in the news.

Previous studies of sourcing reveal disparities in who is included in the news. There is research to suggest that women, for example, are less likely to be included as sources than men (e.g., Mellado & Scherman, 2021; Mitchelstein, Andelsman & Boczkowski, 2019). Black experts are also much less likely to be included as sources (Zeldes & Fico, 2005). In their study of the *St. Louis Dispatch*, for example, Rodgers, Thorson and Antecol (2000) find that "White adult males dominated as sources throughout all sections of the newspaper" (Zeldes & Fico, 2005, 375). Still other work finds that expert sources in particular are also selected based on the prestige of the institutions with which they are affiliated (Armstrong, 2004; McShane, 1995; Powers & Fico, 1994; Zoch & Turk, 1998) – a pattern some have termed "the golden rolodex" (Soley, 1992).

Our work builds on these previous efforts to consider sourcing, with a focus on a particular area of expertise: politics. We begin by tracking the patterns of expert sources in the news, before turning to the driving question of this Element: Whose research and ideas become scientific fact for news audiences?

1.1.1 Layers of Influence

Our approach begins with the idea that media content, as Reese and Shoemaker (2016) write, is a function of different, layered factors such as "individual characteristics of specific newsworkers, their routines of work, organizational-level concerns, institutional issues, and larger social systems" (396) – or what they call the "hierarchy of influences."[1] From our perspective, then, to understand how and why certain experts are included (and, why others are excluded) one must consider not only journalist decision-making and the organizational constraints that shape journalist behavior, but also what Reese and Shoemaker (2016) term "extramedia" influences. Here we consider one particular extramedia factor: the preferences and institutional constraints of the experts themselves.

---

[1] Reeše and Shoemaker (2016) explain these different factors as distinct levels – some micro and some macro.

Constructing expertise through the news operates, at a minimum, under several layers of influence: first, the journalist selects the expert and second, that the expert has the ability and incentive to agree to media requests. While these are necessary conditions for experts to make the news, they simplify what is likely the result of far more complicated interactions between institutions and individuals. Journalists – working under newsroom pressures, within organizational constraints, and under professional norms – select who gets to speak for experts *and* expert preferences. These selections are shaped by the institutional contexts in which journalists and experts operate. Also implied are the sociocultural and professional socialization processes that exert selection effects on both journalists and academics long before they even have the chance to engage in such interactions.

At the end of this interplay between individual preferences and institutional characteristics, the chosen expert source gets the opportunity to define the problem space for the public in a way that could lend certainty to otherwise complex topics. Moreover, the news media are often the primary way the public learns of expertise. Thus, to understand who is included as an expert in the news is to understand how the news informs the public. In other words, who we believe to be an expert and what we believe to be expertise has consequences.

1.1.2 Capturing Expertise in the News

Although different types of individuals can serve as expert sources in the political realm, in this Element we deliberately limit our focus to expert sources with a Ph.D. who are employed by an institution of postsecondary education.[2] We believe our focus on academics as expert sources is both useful and important. First, focusing on academics allows us to define a specific population of expert sources – which gives us greater methodological leverage to track extramedia influences. In Section 4, for example, we conduct a survey of potential sources to better understand how they interact with news media requests – a type of study we could have only done with a defined expert population. Second, academics are often advised to make their work more publicly accessible – "a means of demonstrating impact, as well as a way to help others and inform the public" (Kamau, 2019, 425). From this perspective, interactions between journalists and academics have key implications for *whose* ideas inform. On a broader level, political expertise may be uniquely difficult to convey (Lupia, 2000), and therefore focusing on politics gives us a glimpse into how complex information is cocreated between the experts and the news.

---

[2] Here we include all types of postsecondary institutions.

Finally, there is reason to believe that the patterns we observe with political science academic expert sources can translate to other types of expert sources. While it is outside the scope of this work to investigate whether the patterns we observe for political science extend to other categories of experts, we suspect this may be the case, at least for other social scientific disciplines (e.g., economics, sociology, etc.). We will revisit this point in the Conclusion. There are, undoubtedly, important expert sources who fall outside the academic category; we hope other researchers will extend this work to other expert types and we are hopeful that the findings in this Element can serve as a starting point.

Throughout the Element the goal is, first, to track which types of political experts are most likely to be on journalists' "rosters of expert sources" (Kruvand, 2012, 567). Then, we consider how various individual characteristics of expert sources affect journalists' perceptions of expertise and, ultimately, news judgments.

Who speaks for political experts, our findings suggest, is often a function of who has spoken for political experts in the past. In line with previous research, we also find experts with some social media cachet are more present in the news (McGregor, 2019). And, of course, who had the opportunity to speak in the past is the culmination of other factors – race, gender, and institutional prestige. Ultimately, research on politics is often an area with disagreements – some are conceptual, some are methodological, and some are specific to a particular research area. Thus, people who are elevated to the role of expert sources, especially those who are elevated to that role with frequency, likely speak to a particular set of findings and a particular research agenda. Yet the translation from expert to news means that these ideas become entrenched, often with more certainty than the research suggests. Thus, while the inclusion of expert sources may seem like yet another aspect of news production, it is an aspect with consequences that stretch beyond a single story.

1.2 Who Is an Expert Source?

Before we can understand how and why certain academics end up as expert sources, we need to describe political expert sources and who sources them. Previous projects have examined patterns in the number of official sources cited (Powers & Fico, 1994; Sigel, 1973), and the number of women sourced (Jia et al., 2016; Shor et al., 2015), including the gargantuan task of tracking women sources around the world and across mediums (Macharia, 2020). Other work has considered the role of academic prestige in sourcing, suggesting that scholars from certain types of universities and those who publish in certain types of journals are more likely to be expert sources (Soley, 1992). Indeed,

Soley (1992) blamed journalists' use of a "golden rolodex," or a contact list of expert sources with prestigious credentials (e.g., association with an Ivy League university), for the overrepresentation of academic prestige in the news.

Building on this work, we also begin by considering patterns in expertise by analyzing which types of scholars appear as experts in media coverage. Here, we turn to a content analysis of a random sample of articles published in the *New York Times* during the 2020 national election. Using these articles, we consider whose voices are amplified and elevated to "expert" status. We use this data to consider not only which scholars form the "pictures in our heads" but also which ideas construct our politics.

1.2.1 Methods

We first collected a population of articles the *New York Times* published between August 3, 2020, and November 3, 2020 (Election Day), which contained academics cited as expert sources.[3] Although the *New York Times* is only one source, we follow previous research in treating it as an exemplar outlet (Boydstun, 2013). To start, we collected articles that included *any* expert sources. Although our interest is in political expertise specifically, our goal in the content analysis is to first track the general use of expert sources and then compare these general patterns to the use of political expert sources, specifically. In total, we began with a population of 1,481 articles.

As a next step, we relied on a group of four coders to hand-code a random sample of 901 articles, of which, 556 met our criteria for coding: inclusion of an academic expert source in the form of a stand-alone article or op-ed (rather than, for example, an aggregated news brief or an announcement).[4] Here we further define "expert sources" as those experts included in an article because of their research and knowledge on a topic. By this definition, an academic who was interviewed because of their specific involvement in the topic of the article (e.g., as a plaintiff in a court case or a witness to a crime) would not be considered an expert source, while an academic providing contextual commentary

---

[3] Articles were pulled for the *New York Times* between August 3, 2020, and November 3, 2020, with the key terms "researcher" or "professor" using MediaCloud Explorer. These key terms were decided upon after an iterative process found them to be the most reliable and valid (McGregor et al., n.d.). MediaCloud yielded a list of 1,480 URLs, of which the story text for each was pulled via a Python loop, using the Goose3 package, which extracts articles' content, and metadata from the URL.

[4] To develop the codebook, we followed an iterative process relying on actual *New York Times* content to validate the instrument. After drafting the codebook, we deployed the draft instrument in several rounds of coding practice. We then solicited feedback, using this feedback to further refine the instrument. Once finalized, coders were asked to familiarize themselves with the instrument and were then trained over the course of several hours. Coders participated in several practice rounds of coding to ensure conceptual alignment.

(perhaps based on their research) about a news event would be. In most cases, this took the form of an interview with a journalist; in more rare cases, this took the form of a mention (often with a link) to a research product (e.g., a book, academic article, or survey).[5] The instructions provided to the coders for identifying expert sources are in Online Appendix A.1. This final set of 556 articles included a total of 1,074 expert sources, of whom 976 were unique (some experts were interviewed for multiple articles in our sample).

These articles and experts were first hand-coded for (a) the gender of the journalist and (b) the academic research area of the expert. Again, for the purposes of this Element, experts are defined as individuals with a Ph.D. who are affiliated with an institution of higher education. This definition, of course, limits our discussion and our coding, but does allow us to focus on a defined population, which is critical to the "expert-side" analyses we conduct in Section 4. To retain consistency in coding the research area, coders considered whether the expert was identified as being in a political science department (or teaching a political science course) or in an "adjacent" department – for example, public policy or international relations. If the scholar's departmental affiliation was unclear, coders would search for more information. Any interviewed expert with a political science Ph.D. (or a Ph.D. in an area such as public policy or international relations) would also be considered a political expert regardless of the particular department with which they were affiliated.[6]

When the source's expertise was in politics, the original coders collected additional information, including their gender, institutional affiliation, departmental affiliation, and professional rank. A different coder later hand-collected information on the race of the political sources. Although the political experts were hand-coded, we did obtain demographic information on the remaining experts (i.e., those who were not experts in politics) using software tracking race and gender by name (Imai & Khanna, 2016; Wais, 2015).[7] At a later point, a different coder also collected information on the political experts' social

---

[5] It is possible for an academic to have a byline in the *New York Times*. We do not consider these bylines in our expert source count as they are not a function of journalistic sourcing. An academic with a byline may have been invited to contribute by the editor or they may have pitched the piece themselves; our focus is on journalists (and op-ed writers) selecting expert voices. It is possible for there to be a piece written by an academic that references other academic expert sources; if this was the case, we would have coded those expert sources as usual, but flagged that piece within the analysis. This is not something that occurs within the data.

[6] So, for example, a scholar with a public policy Ph.D. affiliated with an informatics department would be coded as a political expert.

[7] We calculated inter-coder reliability statistics for latent variables coded by separate coders using Krippendorff's alpha. These include (1) whether the article is an opinion piece: $\alpha = 0.72$; (2) gender of the journalist: $\alpha = 0.76$; and (3) number of expert sources: $\alpha = 0.71$.

Table 1 Demographic characteristics, expert sources

	All	All, 1+ Interview	Political	Political, 1+ Interview
Women	37.09%	38.92%	26.73%	22.00%
Men	62.07%	59.88%	73.26%	78.00%
Black	3.54%	3.59%	7.94%	4.00%
Latinx	2.61%	3.59%	1.06%	0
Asian	9.60%	13.17%	10.05%	22.00%
White	83.69%	79.64%	79.31%	74.00%
N	1,073	187	167	50

Note: *N* reflects the number of expert sources.

media presence (whether they were on Twitter and their number of followers), as well as more specific information about their research area.

1.2.2 Broad Patterns in Expertise

As an initial step, we consider overall demographic patterns in our data, starting with the entire set of expert sources, before moving on to the expert sources who study politics. We present these results in Table 1. In these results, the race and gender identifications for the full set of sources are obtained via software (Imai & Khanna, 2016; Wais, 2015), while the race and gender patterns for political expert sources are hand-coded.[8]

Echoing previous research, this first set of results shows that the experts – whether political or otherwise – in our sample are largely men. Notably, the gap between women and men political experts is double the gap between women and men experts, writ large. In the case of political experts, we can compare this percentage to a baseline – the proportion of registered members of the American Political Science Association (APSA) who identify as women. Notably, the proportion of women who are registered members of APSA is 37.4%, suggesting that women are underrepresented in our list of political expert sources.[9] Our sample of experts is also overwhelmingly white. Indeed, 53.6% of the expert

---

[8] Following Imai and Khanna (2016), for racial identification we use the group with the highest produced probability. Note, however, that we deviate slightly from Imai and Khanna (2016) by not using partisan identification. We also used our set of hand-coded experts to consider the validity of the automated coding; using *genderizeR* replicates hand-coding 94% of the time. Predicting race via names predicted the same race as our hand-coded sample 86.9% of the time.

[9] Data from February 2020, reported by APSA here: www.apsanet.org/RESOURCES/Data-on-the-Profession/Dashboard/Membership.

sources in our sample are white men – a proportion that increases to 62.4% in the set of political experts. In contrast, only 4.2% of the political experts in our *New York Times* sample are Black women.

We do not, however, see substantively large shifts in demographics when we consider expert sources who were interviewed more than once (e.g., were quoted in multiple articles) in our sample. In other words, the demographics of experts who gave more than one interview are generally similar to those who only appear once in our sample.

As a next step, we take article-level dynamics into account and consider patterns in expertise as a condition of journalist demographics. Here we focus on the gender of the journalist, which was hand-coded. Some of the articles in our sample were authored by multiple journalists, so we distinguish between articles that had *any* women authors versus those that were authored by men only.[10] We present our results in Table 2.

Previous research suggests that, theoretically, women journalists may be somewhat more likely to include women as expert sources (Hanusch & Nölleke, 2019), though past content analyses do not find a clear relationship between journalist and source gender (Cann & Mohr, 2001). We see that articles that have at least one woman as an author are more likely to include women as expert sources. This is true within the entire sample of articles, as well as in the articles with political expert sources.[11]

As a final step, we consider whether articles with more sources are more likely to have a diverse set of experts simply because the journalists may be reaching out to more people. We see no evidence that this is the case. In fact, we see evidence that the diversity of experts interviewed actually *decreases* as an article features more sources. There are several possible reasons for this outcome. First, articles with multiple expert sources often included coauthors on research projects, and academic networks are likely to be homogeneous (e.g., Teele & Thelen, 2017). Another possibility is that, when journalists work

---

[10] Articles that were written by a group – like the *New York Times* board – are excluded from these results.

[11] While previous research suggests sourcing patterns by gender, there is not clear guidance on what (if any) expectations we can have regarding the interaction of journalist gender and source race. We present the data here for interested readers, hoping it may motivate future study, but caution interpretation accordingly. Some noteworthy patterns: while 48.1% of articles reported by women include sources who are white men, the proportion of white men sources increases to 60.7% in articles written only by men reporters. Although the proportion of Black women as expert sources is very low across all types of articles, Black women are somewhat more likely to be included in articles with at least one woman author. In total, 2.26% of articles authored by at least one woman include Black women as expert sources compared to 0.9% of articles authored only by men. The difference, however, does not reach conventional levels of statistical significance at $p = 0.085$, two-tailed.

Table 2 Demographic characteristics of expert sources, by journalist gender

	All		Political	
	Women journ.	**Men journ.**	**Women journ.**	**Men journ.**
Women	43.62%	28.44%	31.39%	23.23%
Men	55.74%	70.44%	68.60%	76.77%
N	619	450	89	99

Note: *N* reflects the number of expert sources.

on articles with many sources they build their roster of experts by asking already-interviewed experts for recommendations. Again, then, the potential homogeneity of academic networks would lead to a less diverse set of expert sources.

1.2.3 Expertise in Political News

Our goal, however, is to consider the construction of *political* expertise. Therefore, we next turn to patterns in the set of articles interviewing political experts. Here, in addition to demographic variables, we can consider other descriptive information about the scholars. As Table 1 already showed, most of the political expert sources are white and men (indeed, 62.4% of them are white men). As a next step, we turn to their academic backgrounds.

First, unsurprisingly, most political experts interviewed are in political science departments (85.2%). Second, 25.9% of them are from institutions outside the United States. The scholars from international institutions are more likely to have been included as an expert source in more than one article in our sample. The patterns hint at the possibility that once journalists speak to an international expert source they tend to return to that source for other articles that address the same topic, rather than cultivating new international sources.

Next, the plurality of our experts – 45.6% – are scholars of American elections or public opinion; another 13.4% focus on American institutions. This is to be expected given that our sampling frame is articles published in the lead-up to the 2020 election. Comparatively, 16.8% of the political experts are scholars of international relations and 15.4% study elections and public opinion in other countries.

As a next step, we turn to the academic backgrounds of these scholars. Previous research suggests that journalists may be attracted to institutional prestige (Soley, 1992). Therefore, it is reasonable to expect that this preference may manifest in the numbers of expert sources from highly ranked institutions and

Table 3 Academic positions, political expert sources

	All	**1+Interview**
Ph.D. candidate	2.14%	0
Post-doc	0.71%	0
Lecturer	3.57%	0
Assistant	9.29%	0
Associate	21.43%	16.67%
Full	56.43%	83.33%
Emeritus	3.57%	0
N	140	36

Note: International scholars are not included. Percentages do not add to 100% in some cases because either the position of the academic was unclear (0.71%), or the person is deceased (1.43%).

departments in our data. We can extrapolate this idea to professional rank, which can serve as another signal journalists use to select among possible expert sources. In our next set of results, we turn to the positions of our expert sources (e.g., assistant, associate, or full professor) and the ranks of their institution and department. Notably, we can only do so for academics who are within the United States, as both position and rank may not translate globally. We first look at academic positions in Table 3.

The results in Table 3 suggest that the majority of political experts in our sample are full professors. Moreover, full professors are also more likely to be sourced in more than one article. This reliance on full professors may also explain the demographic patterns in Table 1: most full professors in political science are white men (Alter et al., 2020).

We next turn to university ranks – again focusing on American postsecondary education institutions to ensure comparability. First, we note that the bulk of the political experts in our sample – 73.6% – came from R1 institutions.[12] The next largest group of scholars, 7.86%, came from liberal arts colleges. In contrast, only one of the experts in our sample of political sources came from a historically Black college or university.

In Table 4 we present patterns by two types of ranks: the ranking of the political expert's university and the ranking of the political expert's department. We focus here on university rankings given the institutional makeup of the

---

[12] Also classified as Doctoral: Very High Research by the Carnegie Classification of Institutions of Higher Education.

Table 4 Department and university rank, political expert sources

	University		Department	
	All	**1+ Interview**	**All**	**1+ Interview**
Top 10	27.86%	19.44%	23.20%	21.21%
11–30	25.00%	30.56%	17.60%	27.27%
31–50	10.71%	25.00%	23.20%	33.33%
51–70	6.43%	13.89	9.60%	12.12%
71–100	12.14%	11.11%	1.60%	0
101 +	17.86%	0	0.80%	0
No Ph.D. dept.	–	–	25.00%	6.06
N	140	36	125	33

Note: *N* reflects the number of expert sources.

sample. In the departmental rank results – to ensure comparability – we limit our analysis to source experts who are in political science departments.

The patterns in Table 4 suggest that there are higher numbers of political experts from both the top thirty universities and top thirty political science departments. The effects are especially pronounced when we consider experts who have more than one interview in our sample – although, notably, the total number of experts in this group is small. We can conceive of these patterns in another way, focusing on the institutions that are most likely to repeat in our set of political experts (Table 5).

The results in Table 5 add more nuance to these patterns. The institutions with the most expert appearances in our sample are all universities and universities engaged in research (i.e., R1 universities). Indeed, the university appearing most frequently in our sample is Harvard. At the same time, these are not all Ivy League universities; in fact, among American universities they represent a relative range of ranks. What is most notable, however, is that the universities in Table 5 suggest that journalists are returning not simply to the same institutions, but to the same *people*.

1.2.4 Social Media Presence of Political Expert Sources

Shifting away from the academic background of the sources in our sample, we turn to their social media presence, focusing specifically on Twitter. Previous research suggests that journalists look to Twitter for potential sources (McGregor, 2019), and that people who receive a lot of engagement on the platform may be mentioned in editorial meetings (Krupnikov & Ryan, 2022). Thus, it is

Table 5 Universities with multiple appearances in political expert sample

University	Mentions	Unique experts
Harvard University	8	6
Johns Hopkins University	6	6
University of Florida	6	2
American University	5	4
Duke University	5	3
Queen Mary, University of London	4	1
Renmin University	4	2
University of California – Riverside	5	3
University of California – Irvine	4	1
University of Chicago	4	4
University of Michigan	4	4
University of Wisconsin – Madison	4	2

Note: Includes institutions with four or more mentions.

likely that Twitter presence and influence acts as an extra-institutional means to credential potential expert sources.

The political experts included in our sample of *New York Times* articles are more likely to be men and more likely to be senior. The majority of these individuals (59.9%) are also on Twitter.[13] One way to consider Twitter presence is via Twitter followers. Among the political experts interviewed by the *New York Times* (who are on Twitter), the number of followers ranges from 44 to 91,800; the median number of followers is 4,299. Still, it is difficult to understand what this distribution means without additional context. Therefore, we turn to data collected by Bisbee et al. (2020), which includes the number of followers for 1,236 Twitter users in Ph.D.-granting political science departments. We will use this data as a baseline of comparison to the Twitter followers among our sample of political source experts. We present these results in Figure 1.

The first set of results (Figure 1a) present a comparison between the distribution of followers in the Bisbee et al. (2020) data in comparison to the distribution of followers among those political experts sourced by the *New York Times*. These results suggest political expert sources featured by the *New York Times* – at the point of data collection – have more Twitter followers compared to other political scientists.

---

[13] Of this group, 13.83% are "verified" on Twitter.

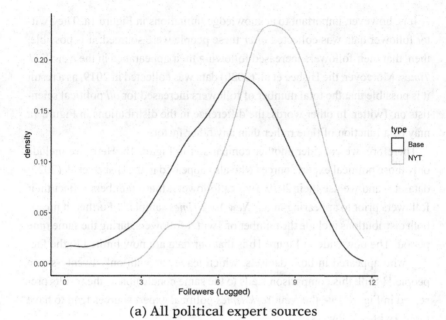

(a) All political expert sources

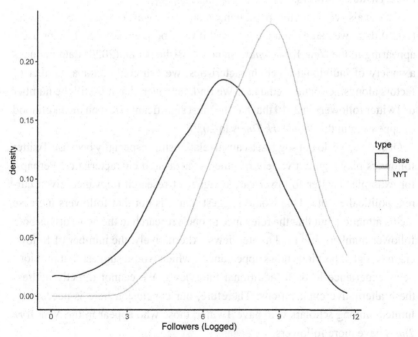

(b) Sources matched to Bisbee et al. (2020),
2019 followers

Figure 1 Distribution of Twitter followers among political expert sources,
relative to a baseline

It is, however, important to acknowledge limitations in Figure 1a. The Twitter follower data was collected *after* these people were sourced; it is possible, then, that their followers increased following their appearance in the *New York Times*. Moreover, the Bisbee et al. (2020) data was collected in 2019, as a result it is possible that the total number of followers increased for *all* political scientists on Twitter. In other words, the difference in the distributions in Figure 1a may be a function of time rather than any other factor.

Therefore, we consider another comparison in Figure 1b. Here, we include only those political expert sources who also appeared in the Bisbee et al. (2020) dataset – and we use their 2019 Twitter followers; these numbers reflect their followers prior to appearing in our *New York Times* sample.[14] Further, it means both distributions include the number of Twitter followers during the same time period. The downside to Figure 1b is that our data are now limited to the faculty who appeared in both datasets, which leaves us with only twenty-seven people.[15] Still, this comparison leads to the same conclusion as the results presented in Figure 1a – the *New York Times* political expert sources tend to have more Twitter followers.

We can also consider this pattern in yet one more way. Using the Bisbee et al. (2020) data, we can estimate the probability of political science Twitter users appearing in the *New York Times*. Since the Bisbee et al. (2020) data includes a variety of individual-level characteristics, we can control for a number of factors alongside social media use. We find, however, that it is still the number of Twitter followers in 2019 that has the most significant effect on the likelihood of appearing in the *New York Times* in 2020.

Of course, we do not suggest a causal relationship, especially because Twitter followers may signal a variety of other, unmeasured characteristics. Perhaps, for example, Twitter followers are a signal of research relevance given current political events. This would suggest that it is not that followers increase media attention, but that the relevance of one's research to the news drives both follower numbers and media interviews. Alternatively, the number of followers may signal previous news appearances, which would suggest that previous news experience leads to additional interviews. We cannot directly address these alternative explanations. Therefore, our conclusion here is necessarily limited: among scholars who have Twitter, those who appear in the *New York Times* have more followers.

---

[14] It is, of course, possible that these experts had already appeared in the *New York Times* at that point.

[15] The Bisbee et al. (2020) data only includes faculty at Ph.D.-granting institutions in the United States.

1.2.5 Tracking Expertise

Our content analysis of the *New York Times* articles shows that political expert sources were more likely to be white, men (and white men), full professors with more Twitter followers than the typical political science professor. Although we do see some variance in the types of institutions these sources represent, most are at R1 universities. These data underscore a long tradition of work in journalistic sourcing that shows a bias toward white men at certain types of academic institutions (Armstrong, 2004; McShane, 1995; Powers & Fico, 1994; Zoch & Turk, 1998) – the "golden rolodex" (Soley, 1992).

The persistence of these patterns in expert sources, however, does not explain why they exist in the first place. Moreover, our goal in this Element is to consider the journalistic decision-making that underlies the construction of expertise. We use the patterns we see in this section to motivate the next sections: If the "golden rolodex" exists, is its existence due to a series of deliberate choices made by journalists? Or is it a byproduct of the various constraints under which journalists operate as they produce the news?

1.3 Overview and Approach

Keeping in mind the demographics of expert sources, in Section 2 we investigate journalistic decision-making using two experiments. The first tracks when journalists perceive research as newsworthy, focusing on the intersection of research content and researcher demographics. The second study relies on a conjoint design, tracking which expert characteristics are most likely to affect sourcing. These two studies point to an idea that is at odds with our findings in Section 1: in the abstract, journalists seem drawn to women and people of color as expert sources.

With the goal of reconciling the results in Section 1 and Section 2, Section 3 focuses on journalists' experiences with *actual* expert sources – since Section 2 dealt in hypotheticals. Turning to a third sample of journalists, we first ask about their "ideal" sources. Then, we ask them to recall their most recent expert sources. The results of these two tasks – unlike the patterns in Section 2 – are more in line with the demographic profiles of expert sources we find in Section 1.

In Section 4, we attempt to understand this difference between actual patterns and abstract goals in expert sourcing by addressing possible "supply-side" explanations. To this end, we turn to the experts themselves; specifically, we conduct a survey of political science faculty. This survey lends nuance to the previous sections and to our understanding of expertise in the news broadly, which we discuss in Section 5. Journalists, we find, are drawn to diverse expert sources – they want to speak to women and people of color. Yet, despite these preferences, in daily life when facing real-world constraints, journalists are more likely to include white men as expert sources.

Ultimately, then, our findings suggest a complicated portrait of expertise – a process that is reflective of a "hierarchy of influences" (Reese & Shoemaker, 2016; Shoemaker & Reese, 2014). On an individual level, as we will show in Section 2, journalists may prefer more diverse sources. At the same time, however, they may be constrained by institutional and organizational factors, which likely leads journalists to return to experts they have interviewed in the past. If the "golden rolodex" exists, it exists in part because journalists often work quickly and rely on signals of prestige. Underlying these patterns are what Reese and Shoemaker (2016) term "extramedia" influences – the broader social context and academic institutions that disproportionately credential experts who are white, and men. Indeed, the disparities we see in our content analysis of expert sources in this section replicate the disparities that we see in political science departments (and, likely, academe at large).

2 How Journalists Select Experts

2.1 What Drives Journalistic Sourcing?

What explains the demographic patterns we see in our audit of political experts in the *New York Times* in Section 1? Namely, what explains the fact that political expert sources are more likely to be white, men with larger than average Twitter followings, at R1 universities? Sources anchor news frames, dictating the way a story is constructed (Tuchman, 1972). Source selection also influences what information is considered relevant to a story (Reese & Shoemaker, 2016), and the tilt of a story (Coddington & Molyneux, 2021; Steiner, 2012). For this reason, the selection of sources is one of the most important components of the news-making process (Jörgen & Folke, 1994; Zoch & Turk, 1998).

It is the journalist's perception of a source's newsworthiness that drives the likelihood they'll be included in the article, rather than the actual information exchanged (Carlson, 2009). Source newsworthiness judgments are driven by the same calculus that affects the selection of stories; decision-making guided by news values (Gans, 1979). News values are newsworthiness criteria, imbued through journalism education and professional socialization, that journalists use to sort the stories that rise to the level of news from those that do not (Galtung & Ruge, 1965). News values include conflict, drama, human interest, relevance, and proximity (Harcup & Deirdre, 2016). One way to satisfy these criteria is to select exclusive, elite, or high-status sources (Weaver et al., 2009), a tendency demonstrated in journalistic preference for official sources (Ferré, 1996; Powers & Fico, 1994; Schlesinger, 1990). For professional and economic reasons, journalists are also attracted to authority (Bourdieu, 2001; Djerf-Pierre, 2007; Steiner, 2012). Another way to satisfy these criteria is to select sources that are dynamic, assertive, accessible, or quotable. Previous work finds that such source characteristics affect the prominence and dominance of their quotes (Gans, 1979; Stempel & Culbertson, 1984).

Sourcing selection is also affected by newsroom constraints: without the time and resources required, journalists must seek sources that are convenient, available, and useful. Indeed, expert sources act as information subsidies, mitigating uncertainty (Brown et al., 1987; Gandy, 1982). As inclusion of expert sources affects perceptions of news credibility, an important consideration for journalists, it is strategic to select experts who are indisputably authoritative on their subject area. Since journalists, like most people, have been socialized to see male-dominated fields like academia as inherently masculine (Eagly & Karau, 2002), it is unsurprising that men are more likely to be selected as news sources, even above and beyond their proportion of the workforce (McShane, 1995), and even in domains dominated by women (Blumell, 2017), regardless of the increasing number of women in the newsroom (Ross et al., 2016).

Moreover, the role of expert sources as protective factors, reducing uncertainty in areas wherein journalists lack expertise, makes it unlikely that journalists will seek experts perceived as outside the norm (Lewis et al., 2008). And, looking at the expert sources that make it to the news, our work – and the work of many others – demonstrate that women sources remain outside the norm (Macharia, 2020), despite the fact that women sources are viewed as no less credible (Paul, Sui & Searles, 2021). This same logic extends to other patterns we see in our data: the rank of full professor and employment at R1 universities are all signals that credential a person (Berlo, Lemert & Mertz, 1969; Day & Golan, 2005).

Source selection is one of the few editorial decisions firmly within the journalist's purview (Zoch & Turk, 1998). As a result, uncovering mechanisms at work in journalistic source selection may reveal biases that affect news-making (Barnoy & Reich, 2020). Because it is unlikely that a conscious preference for any one source characteristic is made known in the selection process (Weaver et al., 2009), it is all the more important to understand if and when characteristics of expert sources affect journalistic sourcing practices. Therefore, we use experiments to consider these selection dynamics, harnessing the power of randomization to shed light on aspects of journalistic decision-making that may not be evident to even the journalists themselves. Since experiments are rarely used in the study of journalism – for a variety of technological and methodological reasons – these data give us a rare glimpse into how journalists make decisions about expertise.

2.2 Source Gender and Newsworthiness

As discussed in the previous section, the perceived newsworthiness of the source motivates journalistic selection. As perceptions of source credibility and information credibility are tightly coupled in journalist decision-making (Barnoy & Reich, 2020), judgments of newsworthiness and perceived expertise may also be related. Journalists have significant discretion over newsworthiness judgments, a step which occurs early in the news-making process. As a result, we can leverage an experimental context to manipulate characteristics of experts and assess subsequent newsworthiness judgments to investigate the extent to which these judgments affect expert source selection. In other words, we can look for systematic variation in the *types* of experts journalists deem newsworthy to better understand the expert sourcing patterns we saw in Section 1.

As a first step, we begin with an experiment that considers whether researcher gender affects the extent to which journalists find their research newsworthy. In a second experiment we will broaden our analysis to characteristics besides researcher gender (including their race, academic institution, and social media presence), to track more detailed patterns in source selection.

2.2.1 Study 1: Expert Source Gender and Perceptions of Newsworthiness

In this experiment, our goal was to track journalists' perceptions of newsworthiness in an unobtrusive way. Therefore, in Study 1 we ask journalists to rank a series of five vignettes that detail research findings from least to most newsworthy. All five vignettes were obtained from the "News & Media" sections of different university websites. To increase believability, we listed the name of the university and framed the research similarly to the university media professionals. To add to internal validity, we featured only public, Big 10 universities located in the Midwest.

Journalists were randomly assigned to one of six experimental conditions. Across all conditions, journalists were presented with the five research

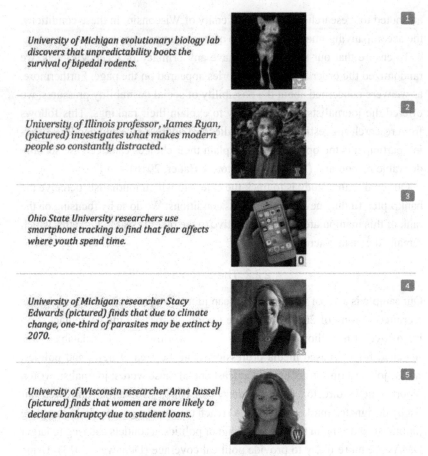

University of Michigan evolutionary biology lab discovers that unpredictability boots the survival of bipedal rodents.

University of Illinois professor, James Ryan, (pictured) investigates what makes modern people so constantly distracted.

Ohio State University researchers use smartphone tracking to find that fear affects where youth spend time.

University of Michigan researcher Stacy Edwards (pictured) finds that due to climate change, one-third of parasites may be extinct by 2070.

University of Wisconsin researcher Anne Russell (pictured) finds that women are more likely to declare bankruptcy due to student loans.

Figure 2 Treatment, Study 1

vignettes; four of the five vignettes remained identical for each journalist (Figure 2), but one vignette – which referred to a researcher from the University of Wisconsin – featured randomized attributes. In one condition, the participants saw a woman named Anne Russell whose research found that women were more likely to declare bankruptcy due to student loans (just as in Figure 2). In another condition, participants saw the same finding, but the researcher named and depicted was a man (Andrew Russell). Two additional conditions also varied researcher gender, but this time Anne/Andrew's research findings reported that it was *men* who were more likely to declare bankruptcy. The final two conditions did not specify the researcher (thus avoiding a gender cue), but simply reported the bankruptcy finding (either for men or women) attributed to "researchers" at the University of Wisconsin. In these conditions, the accompanying image was a photo of a graduation cap.

To ensure that our study did not have any primacy or recency effects, we randomized the order in which the stories appeared on the page. Furthermore, as we were concerned about the possibility of social desirability pressures, we offered the journalists an opportunity to explain their rankings. This follows from research suggesting that – in studies that address race and gender – offering participants the opportunity to explain their choices can decrease socially desirable responding (Krupnikov, Piston & Bauer, 2016)

Our goal in this study is to track the extent to which journalists perceive the bankruptcy finding newsworthy across conditions. We do so by focusing on the rank of this manipulated vignette relative to the other research vignettes which remained constant across conditions.[16]

2.2.2 The Sample

Our sample is a set of working American journalists, N=587. This sample was recruited in May of 2019 through the Cision database, a media contact service of over 1.6 million media professionals worldwide.[17] The database was searched for US-based media professionals in the area of news and politics, whose job descriptions contained at least one of these words: journalist, writer, reporter, news director, correspondent, and editor. We further narrowed our list by designated market area (DMA) reach to ensure we were likely sampling journalists working in the broad domain of politics, as outlets catering to larger DMAs are more likely to provide political coverage (Dunaway, 2013). Using these search terms, our pool of potential participants included 14,548 working journalists who were contacted via email and asked to participate in our study.[18]

---

[16] Although our main study is conducted on a sample of working American journalists, we also fielded the same study on a convenience sample using Amazon Mechanical Turk (MTurk), N=517. In this study, participants were asked what they would find most newsworthy as subscribers to a news website. The full results of this pilot test are included in the Online Appendix B.1.

[17] This database is updated on a daily basis to retain full contact information for people classified as working for a media organization. This feature of the database is important as newsrooms have high rates of turnover, and reliable, person-specific contact information can be difficult to locate on outlet websites. Ambiguous or general outlet emails may be checked by media professionals other than those we hope to speak with, such as interns or employees working in sales and advertising.

[18] Of the initial email, 101 emails bounced back. Additionally, we conducted a check on our final sample to ensure that our process did produce a sample of the types of individuals we were hoping to study - journalists who focus on politics. We asked journalists to categorize themselves by their primary area of focus. We found that 93.5% self-categorized as being primarily responsible for government and political news.

To increase trust and encourage participation, the survey invite was penned by a former working journalist, and a ten-dollar gift card was offered to a store or charity of choice.[19] The decision to offer a small incentive that included charitable options, and the design of the invite, were informed by personal correspondence with working journalists and journalism experts (Molyneux & Zamith, 2020). Journalists who did not open the original email were sent a follow-up after two weeks. In total, 79.24% of the contacted journalists received reminder emails. Overall, our response rate in the study was 4.8% (using AAPOR RR1) and we had a cooperation rate of 25.1% (using AAPOR Cooperation Rate 1). We note that this response rate is markedly similar to rates reported on specific subpopulations with surveys that rely only on email contact (Petrovčič, Petrič & Manfreda, 2016). Indeed, there is reason to believe that surveys of journalists generally have low response rates even when they come from industry actors (e.g., American Society of Newsroom Editors reports a low response rate for their 2018 survey, for example). Other surveys of journalists conducted online that feature higher response rates often include general (rather than individual) newsroom email accounts, and professional roles outside of news workers (e.g., sales).

In total, our final set of journalists comprised a professionally diverse group. Our sample, for example, ranged from early career journalists (fewer than two years in the profession), to those who had been in the profession for over forty years. Most of these journalists worked for a newspaper, though our sample also included journalists working for television and web-only sources. Many described their assignments largely as local news; 26.5% reported they worked primarily on local news, while 29.4% said they covered general news. The majority of the journalists in our sample identified as men (57.41%).

We include the details of our sample in Table 6, where we also compare the sample to other surveys of journalists (e.g., Molyneux & Zamith, 2020; Willnat, Weaver & Wilhoit, 2017). We see that our demographic patterns on gender come closer to Molyneux and Zamith (2020) than Willnat et al. (2017), likely reflecting the timing of the surveys (Willnat et al. (2017) ran their survey in 2013) and more recent efforts to increase gender diversity in media organizations (e.g., Rattan et al., 2019). We also see some differences in representation of various outlets, but note that part of the difference may be due to the inclusion of different categories in the surveys.

---

[19] To add a layer of security to the process, gift codes for the incentives were disbursed outside the original survey instrument via Rybbon, a secure platform for gifting.

Table 6 Sample characteristics, Study 1

	Study 1, 2019	Willnat et al., 2013	Molyneux and Zamith, 2018
	Demographics		
Men	57.41%	62.5%	55%
Women	42.15%	37.5%	45%
Mean age	47.25 years	–	–
	Professional Background		
Mean years as journalist	22.02 years	21 years	19 years
Attended Journalism school	14.57%	–	–
	Outlet		
Daily newspaper	22.87%	33.14%	–
Weekly newspaper	17.97%	22.03%	
Community newspaper	14.52%	–	–
Television	6.72%	12.22%	–
Radio	6.35%	8.98%	–
News website	12.52%	8.51%	–
News service/syndicate	4.17%	9.54%	–
News magazine	3.27%	5.55%	–
N	551	1,080	642

Note: The years in the first row refer to the date of the survey; the patterns are reported in Molyneux and Zamith (2020) and Willnat et al. (2017). Outlet percentages will not add up to 100% due to participants selecting "other."

2.2.3 Results

We begin with a simple test: What is the average ranking the journalists assign to our manipulated story? In this case, a higher mean means that the story is *less* newsworthy (i.e., it is ranked near or exactly last). We find that, on average, the journalists consider our manipulated research vignette most newsworthy when it features a woman researcher with a result that focuses on women. In fact, this story is considered significantly more newsworthy than the same finding attributed to a man ($p = 0.047$) and significantly more newsworthy than a man with a finding about men ($p = 0.001$).[20] In contrast however, we see less of a difference in newsworthiness between a woman

---

[20] All reported *p*-values are two-tailed.

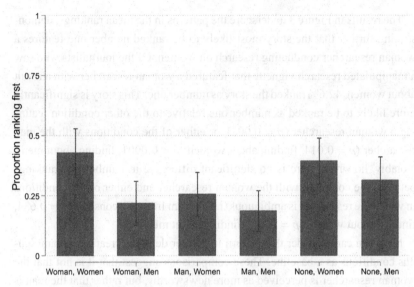

Figure 3 Effect of treatment on ranking, Study 1
The x-axis categories first specify the gender of the researcher, and then specify the gender focus of the findings.

with a finding about women and the same woman with a finding about men ($p = 0.063$). Moreover, there is even less difference between this condition and the two conditions that do not cue gender of the researcher at all.[21]

These results suggest that it is not the research finding that matters most, but the gender of the *researcher*. Therefore, as a next step we simply consider the effect of researcher gender, without accounting for the research finding. The results suggest that the journalists are significantly less likely to see the research as newsworthy when it is conducted by a man ($p = 0.017$). There is, however, no difference in mean newsworthiness between the story in which the researcher is a woman and in which researcher gender is not cued at all ($p = 0.964$).[22]

Although the mean ranking already suggests that research conducted by a woman is perceived as more newsworthy by journalists, we can consider the results in a more intuitive way. To do so, we rank how our treatment affects the proportion of journalists who rank the manipulated research vignette first (most newsworthy), using a binary variable which assigns a 1 to such responses (all else 0). We present the patterns in Figure 3.[23]

---

[21] Full model is included in Online Appendix Table B.2.
[22] Full model is included in Online Appendix Table B.3.
[23] Full model is included in Online Appendix Table B.4.

The results in Figure 3 underscore the patterns in the mean rankings, demonstrating further that the story most likely to be ranked number one features a woman researcher conducting research on women. Of the journalists who saw a manipulated research vignette that featured a woman researcher with a result about women, 42.6% ranked the story as number one. This story is significantly more likely to be ranked as number one relative to the other condition featuring a woman researcher ($p = 0.003$), or either of the conditions with the man researcher ($p = 0.014$, finding about women; $p < 0.0001$, finding about men). Notably, however, there is no significant difference in number one rankings between the condition with the woman researcher and either of the conditions in which the researcher is ambiguous (i.e., "Team from Wisconsin") ($p = 0.634$, finding about women; $p = 0.112$, finding about men).

Next, we can consider this pattern in greater depth by treating the ambiguous conditions as a baseline. These comparisons suggest that it is not that the woman researcher is perceived as more newsworthy, but rather that the man is perceived as significantly *less* newsworthy.[24]

2.2.4 A Puzzling Pattern

The results from the first study seem in sharp contrast to the patterns we uncovered by our content analysis of the *New York Times* in Section 1. The patterns in our content analysis suggest that men vastly outnumber women as expert sources – yet the patterns in Study 1 suggest that journalists are more likely to perceive research by a woman as newsworthy. Perhaps there is an alternative explanation for these results.

In our content analysis, we find, for example, that women journalists are more likely to source women as experts. To test whether journalist gender is a possible driver of these patterns, we analyze our results by gender of the journalist to see if the effect is driven by women journalists. We do so, by interacting our treatments with journalist gender.

We do not find any evidence to this point. In fact, women journalists tend to give slightly lower ratings to the woman researcher than men journalists, but give slightly higher ratings to the man researcher. The main difference between the two groups of journalists is that women journalists are somewhat more drawn to a research finding about women, but men journalists are generally more drawn to the woman researcher. We note however, that none of the gender

---

[24] Comparing the ambiguous researcher and finding about women condition to the condition that features a man as the researcher and a finding about women produces $p = 0.005$. Comparing the ambiguous researcher and finding about men condition to the condition that features a man as the researcher and a finding about men produces $p = 0.004$.

differences reach statistical significance.[25] In sum, journalist gender cannot explain the patterns of newsworthiness perceptions presented in Study 1.

It is also possible that, despite our best attempts to address social desirability, the patterns we find still reflect some socially desirable responding. Another possibility is that the real world sourcing data reflect a more complicated decision calculus that our experiment necessarily lacks. The predominance of men sources in the *New York Times* may be due to source characteristics other than gender, or perhaps a more complex interaction of many characteristics. Still another possibility is that the main measure in Study 1 – newsworthiness – is not capturing the dynamics that lead to source selection. In other words, there may be a difference between the newsworthiness of a source generally and the usefulness of a source for a particular story. Therefore, as a next step, we turn to a second study, now with a different sample of journalists. In this second study, we will rely on a conjoint experimental design to map sourcing decisions with more causal precision. The different factors included in the conjoint, we believe, also address any lingering concerns regarding the potential for social desirability, while allowing us to consider a broader set of source characteristics beyond gender.

2.3 Study 2: Conjoint Analysis of Journalistic Source Preferences

In the conjoint experiment, respondents were shown two different potential expert sources and asked which they would prefer to interview for "an article in the general area of American politics." The respondents were given seven attributes of the potential sources. Two attributes are demographic characteristics: gender, and race. Two attributes relate to their professional status: number of citations, and the type of postsecondary education institution that currently employs them.[26] Two relate to their Twitter profile: how many followers they have, and how many tweets they have sent. Finally, they are also told about the source's previous experience with media interviews. We list the full set of attributes and levels in Table 7. The respondents participated in two decision rounds. The order of characteristics was randomly assigned to each participant, but remained constant across both rounds (following Bansak et al., 2021). Thus, the analysis accounts for multiple observations on the same respondent.

This study relies on a second sample of journalists, different from the sample discussed in Study 1. This new sample ($N = 223$) was recruited in November

---

[25] Full model is included in Online Appendix Table B.5.

[26] Citation levels based on data collected by Peress (2019); Twitter levels based on follower and tweet information collected by Bisbee et al. (2020).

Table 7 Expert source attributes and levels, Study 2

Attribute	Levels	Attribute	Levels
1. Gender		5. Twitter followers	
	• Man		• 240
	• Woman		• 1729
			• 7150
2. Race		6. Tweets	
	• Asian		• 143
	• Black		• 721
	• Latinx		• 2809
	• White		
3. Citations		7. Experience	
	• 329		• No previous experience
	• 1,114		• Interviews with national outlets
	• 3,119		• Interviews with local outlets only
4. Institution			
	• Community college		
	• Large public		
	• Large private		
	• Liberal arts		
	• Ivy League		

2021 using the same methods as the first study.[27] Given this similarity, we do not repeat recruitment details here. Sample characteristics are in Table 8, again alongside patterns from previous surveys for reference.

2.3.1 Results

When analyzing the results of the experiment, we estimate the average marginal component effects (AMCE) which have a direct causal interpretation. For each

---

[27] Response rate was 5.7 percent. To calculate this rate, we exclude emails that were not deliverable either for technical reasons or individual-specific reasons (e.g., journalist no longer employed by the outlet). Importantly, high turnover rates in the profession are one of the reasons that we opted to use the Cision database (which is consistently updated) instead of assembling a contact list manually. Of those who opened the email, we have a cooperation rate of 17.5 percent.

Table 8 Sample characteristics, Study 2

	Study 2, 2021	Willnat et al., 2013	Molyneux and Zamith, 2018
	Demographics		
Men	52.31%	62.5%	55%
Women	47.22%	37.5%	45%
Mean age	42.82 years	–	–
	Professional background		
Mean years as journalist	18.15 years	21 years	19 years
Attended journalism school	16.0%	–	–
	Outlet		
Daily newspaper	50.52%	33.14%	–
Weekly newspaper	10.31%	22.03%	–
Community newspaper	12.89%	–	–
Television	2.06%	12.22%	–
Radio	0	8.98%	–
News website	15.46%	8.51%	–
News service/syndicate	2.58%	9.54%	–
News magazine	1.03%	5.55%	–
N	216	1,080	642

Note: The years in the first row refer to the date of the survey; the patterns are reported in Molyneux and Zamith (2020) and Willnat et al. (2017). Outlet percentages will not add up to 100% due to participants selecting "other."

of the attribute categories, the estimated AMCEs tell us whether a particular attribute in that category makes a respondent more or less likely to choose a source compared to a baseline attribute in that category. Essentially, the interpretation is the same as with a set of dummy variables for a categorical variable in a regression analysis. Because the conjoint experiment is fully randomized (with no constraints), we can say that any differences we observe compared to the baseline are causally related to a preference on the part of the respondents, on average. For example, on the citations attribute, the two potential source experts could be described as having 329, 1,114, or 3,119 citations. The analysis tells us whether having 1,114 or 3,119 cites makes a respondent more or less likely to source that expert than if they had 329 citations (the baseline).

One of the benefits of a conjoint experiment is that it has been shown to reduce socially desirable responding (Bansak et al., 2021; Horiuchi, Markovich

& Yamamoto, 2021). This feature of the design is important as social desirability responding is one possible explanation for why we see few women experts in our *New York Times* content analysis, and yet an expressed preference for newsworthy women experts in Study 1. In Study 1, social desirability may have led the journalists to over-report the extent to which they perceive the woman as newsworthy. In the conjoint analysis, however, the source descriptions using multiple characteristics may offer journalists more "cover" for selecting men. Further, the structure of the conjoint will allow us to track which characteristics the journalists use when comparing sources. If the AMCE for gender, for example, is not statistically different from 0 but experience and citations are statistically greater than 0, then journalists are unlikely to consider gender when making choices, but they are likely to consider experience and citations.

We plot the results in Figure 4. Looking first at the demographic attributes at the top of the figure, we see that journalists in the experiment tend to choose women experts more frequently than men experts and choose white experts less frequently than sources of any other race. There are no differences among non-white sources. Given one of the purposes of the conjoint is to overcome social desirability, this suggests journalists actually prefer any source over a white man – which, of course, is noteworthy given the ubiquity of white men experts in the media. This is an important result that bears additional discussion, and we will return to it later.

When we look at the effects of experts' institutional affiliation on source selection, we see that all institutional categories, with the exception of the Ivy League, are statistically different from the baseline, community college. The other categories are not different from each other, however. In an additional analysis, we split the sample between men and women reporters and find that these results are driven entirely by men (see Online Appendix B.3, Figure 6, for full results). There are no statistically significant effects of institutional affiliation for women reporters, but men prefer all of the postsecondary education institutional types (large public and private universities, liberal arts colleges, and Ivy League universities) to community colleges. To get more understanding of what is happening, we looked at the marginal means, that is, the probability that an expert with a particular attribute is likely to be chosen (Horiuchi, Markovich & Yamamoto, 2020). What we observe is that the effect occurs because men are not interested in experts who work at community colleges – these experts are chosen only about one-quarter of the time. The marginal means for almost all the other institutional categories overlap with 0.5, suggesting they are not a factor in the journalist's decision-making.

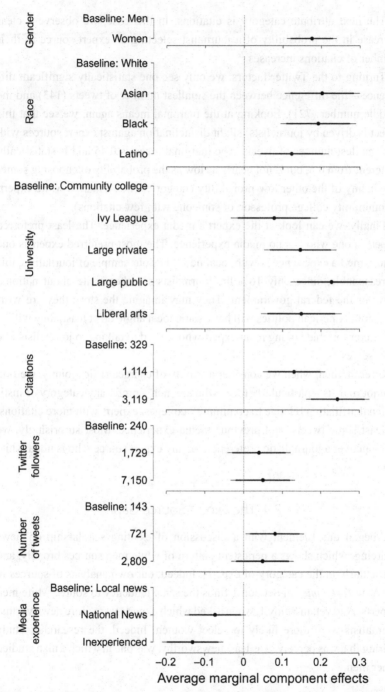

Figure 4 Average effect of expert characteristics on source selection, Study 2
Features 95% Confidence Intervals.

The next attribute category is citations. In this case, we observe a clear increase in the probability of a journalist selecting an expert source as their number of citations increases.[28]

Turning to the Twitter factors, we only see one statistically significant difference – the difference between the smallest number of tweets (143) and the middle number (721). Looking at the marginal means again, we see that this effect is driven by journalists' slight disinclination against expert sources with the smallest number of tweets. The marginal mean is 0.45 and is statistically different from 0.5, but is not nearly as low as the probability of choosing someone in any of the other low-probability categories (i.e., a man, a white expert, a community college professor, or someone with few citations).

Finally, we can look at the expert's media experience. The least preferred expert is one who has no media experience. The most preferred expert is one whose media experience is with local news. For our sample of journalists, this is reasonable, since only 16% the journalists say they write about national news or the federal government. They may imagine the story they are writing about American politics will have some local angle or, at least, they will be more comfortable talking to an expert who is used to talking to journalists like themselves.

Overall, then, when we consider a variety of characteristics jointly, we find that journalists – particularly those who are men – prefer any category of institutional affiliation relative to community colleges, experts with more citations, at least some tweets, and previous media experience. Most surprisingly, we also uncover a journalistic preference for any expert source who is not a white man.

2.4 The Expert Source Gap

We began this Element with a discussion of existing scholarship on news sourcing, which shows a persistent pattern of white men sources broadly, and particularly in the category of experts. Indeed, our own analysis of sources in the *New York Times* in Section 1 finds the same tendency to source white men experts. And yet, in Study 1, when asked which experts were more newsworthy, journalists were more likely to select women. Indeed, the researcher–study pairing that was perceived as least newsworthy, was one in which a man studied other men.

---

[28] We also find a significant increase in the probability of being chosen between the middle (1,114) and top (3,119) categories of citation counts.

In Study 2, when given an array of possible expert attributes using a conjoint design, journalists were mostly likely to select any expert who is *not* a white man. Moreover, although journalists were less likely to interview a source from a community college, they did not seem to distinguish between the Ivy League and other types of postsecondary education institutions. Since scholars have suggested that a conjoint design decreases social desirability bias (Bansak et al., 2021), these results likely indicate a sincere preference rather than the goal of signaling virtue. If this is the case, however, then why is there a gap between the people journalists actually source and the sources journalists prefer in our studies? To answer this question, in the next section, we turn to a series of studies that move out of the realm of hypotheticals, to better understand real-world sourcing decisions.

3 Demand-Side: Expert Source Characteristics

3.1 Introduction

Both experiments in Section 2 (Study 1 and Study 2) offer us the opportunity to isolate the characteristics of expert sources that motivate journalistic selection. In both studies we find that, when journalists are shown a list of possible expert sources, they tend to gravitate toward women and people of color.

There are two potential limitations to our results thus far. First, the experiments in Section 2 deal in hypotheticals, rather than real sourcing decisions. Second, the patterns in these studies seem to stand in sharp contrast to the results of our content analysis in Section 1. In Section 1, we saw broad gender and race disparities in expert sources in *New York Times* articles, but in Section 2 we see that journalists are drawn to more diverse sources; in Section 1 the most common source group was white men, but in Section 2 journalists seemed least likely to select white men as sources.

One possibility in reconciling these patterns is that when *given* a list of sources journalists gravitate toward diversity, but under time constraints, they tend to return to the same expert sources over and over again. Indeed, time constraints can lead journalists to "rely on a few, readily available sources"(Conway, 2021, 5). Once journalists find sources who are both authoritative and reliable (e.g., Gans, 1979), the incentive is to keep returning to that expert source. Another possibility is that when writing political stories, journalists may be more interested in political topics that are more commonly associated with men, and in topics which men researchers are more likely to study. Jointly, these factors further entrench journalistic sourcing networks that are more likely to include men (Johnson, Steve & Aelst, 2018).

Table 9 Sample characteristics, Study 3 and Study 4

	Studies 3 and 4, 2020	Willnat et al., 2013	Molyneux and Zamith, 2018
	Demographics		
Men	52.39%	62.5%	55%
Women	47.04%	37.5%	45%
Mean age	41.70 years	–	–
	Professional background		
Mean years as journalist	17.12 years	21 years	19 years
Attended journalism school	9.09%	–	–
	Outlet		
Daily newspaper	48.88%	33.14%	-
Weekly newspaper	11.66%	22.03%	–
Community newspaper	14.80%	–	–
Television	2.69%	12.22%	–
Radio	0	8.98%	–
News website	13.45%	8.51%	–
News service/syndicate	0.45%	9.54%	–
News magazine	0	5.55%	–
N	368	1,080	642

Note: The years in first row refer to the date of the survey; the patterns are reported in Molyneux and Zamith (2020) and Willnat et al. (2017). Outlet percentages will not add up to 100% due to participants selecting "other."

In this section we turn to these two ideas: the role of time constraints and networks. Specifically we first consider who comes to mind when journalists are asked to think of political expert sources quickly. Second, we delve into the way journalists think of expert sourcing by relying on a "name-generator" task – the same task used to consider network interactions. Our data in this section come from a third sample of working American journalists, $N = 368$, recruited in December 2020 using the same method described in detail in Section 2, Study 1. Sample characteristics can be found in Table 9.[29] This sample of journalists completed two tasks: the timed study (Study 3) and the name-generator (Study 4).

---

[29] Response rate is 7.6. As we did previously, response rate was calculated to exclude emails that were not deliverable for technical or individual (e.g., employment changed) reasons.

3.2 Study 3: Sourcing under Pressure

In an attempt to explain why we see a lack of diversity in our *New York Times* data, for Study 3 we conduct a test to see if time pressure may be to blame. Do journalists intend to source women and experts of color, but get swamped and rely on their tried and true contacts? To explore this idea, we began by asking our sample of journalists to think of an expert who might be their "ideal source" on a political topic. The journalists were told to focus on academic experts for a political topic of their choice – they would be writing a "feature on politics that includes academic research for context." The journalists were also advised that they would have the time and resources to interview this person.

While all participants received a similar task – think of an ideal academic source – we randomly assigned the *time* in which our participants had to do so. Some journalists had as much time as they needed, while a second group was told that they had only 15 seconds to think of a source. The journalists in this second condition saw a 15 second count-down clock on their screens.

This task is meant to mimic (albeit in a limited fashion) the time pressures journalists feel day-to-day, so that we can test the possibility that such constraints are what affect source diversity. We expect that when given ample time, journalists may be more likely to think of and reach out to sources outside their networks, but in a time-pressured situation they would be likely to go with the first names that came to mind. This latter set of circumstances should be more likely to lead journalists to rely on a more narrow set of expert sources.

Our outcomes in this study are a set of names. Independent coders (unaware of the conditions or the prompts) coded these names for a variety of characteristics – including their gender, the institution in which they worked, the institution in which they received their PhD, their social media presence, and their academic position. In what follows, we consider the patterns of sources by condition.

3.2.1 Results

Of our sample of journalists, some 48% did not offer an expert at all. This proportion was identical across conditions, suggesting that this was not created by random assignment (see Online Appendix C.2).[30] Next, before considering the sources our participants listed, we conduct one more validity check: We compare the time they took to complete the task in each condition. Here we see that those in the untimed condition take significantly longer to respond

---

[30] We do, however, find that women were somewhat more likely not to offer a name in both conditions, see Online Appendix C.2.

($p < 0.001$), suggesting that our treatment did create different decision contexts for the journalists.[31]

Focusing on the journalists who did offer a source, we begin with the most basic result: 78.5% of our journalists offered the name of a man. We see little difference by treatment, though – contrary to our predictions – journalists were somewhat more likely to name a woman as an ideal source in the *timed* condition.[32] We note, however, that in some cases – despite our instructions – the journalists did not offer an academic expert; some journalists, for example, offered expert sources like Hillary Clinton and Steve Kornacki. However, even if we limit our focus only to those journalists offering academic expert sources, we find largely similar patterns. Indeed, if we limit our focus to those who named academic sources we find *no difference* between our two conditions; in both conditions, 77.7% of journalists name academic men.[33] We also note – contrary to the content analysis presented in Section 1 – we see very little difference by the gender of the journalists: Both men and women journalists are equally likely to name men as sources.[34]

For the sake of comparison, we provide additional information for our ideal sources in Table 10, including the same characteristics considered in the content analysis in Section 1: academic position and institutional affiliation. The data show, similarly to Section 1, journalists are more likely to cite ideal sources that are full professors. However, unlike the sources in the *New York Times*, the experts who journalists named as their ideal sources were not as likely to be at a top-30 university. Instead, we see that most sources named are employed by institutions with a ranking of 111 or higher. Whether journalists are under time pressure seems to matter little with regard to these patterns.

Overall, for the journalists in our sample, it seems to be the case that ideal expert sources need not work at prestigious universities. To make it to the pages of the *New York Times*, however, an expert source has a better shot if they are affiliated with a top university. These data, then, suggest different sourcing

---

[31] Mean response time in the timed condition was 8.71 seconds; mean response time in the untimed condition was 53.92 seconds.

[32] In the untimed condition, 81.1% of journalists offered a man as a source, while in the timed condition, 75.4% of journalists named a man as a source.

[33] More precisely: 77.6% in the untimed condition, 77.8% in the timed condition.

[34] If we limit our focus to academics only, 77.4% of men journalists named men in the untimed condition, and 77.1% did so in the timed condition; 77.8% of women journalists named men in the untimed condition and 78.9% did so in the timed condition. If we look at all experts, 75.6% of men journalists named men in the untimed condition, and 78.1% did so in the timed condition; 84.2% of women journalists named men in the untimed condition and 75% did so in the timed condition.

Table 10 Academic backgrounds of ideal
political expert sources, Study 3

	Untimed	Timed
	Position	
Lecturer	5.26%	7.55%
Assistant	1.75%	3.77%
Associate	14.04%	5.66%
Full	68.42%	73.58%
Emeritus or other	10.53%	9.43%
	Institutional rank	
Top 10	6.90%	7.55%
11–30	15.52%	20.37%
31–50	10.34%	5.56%
51–70	8.62%	11.11%
71–90	3.45%	5.56%
91–110	1.72%	3.70%
111+	53.45%	44.44%

Note: The "lecturer" category includes all listed
individuals who are not tenured or tenure track.
In most of these cases, these individuals are not
adjuncts.

motivations between reporters at the *New York Times* and the journalists in our
sample.

Next we consider the idea that it is journalists' networks, or their roster of
expert sources, that are to blame for a lack of source diversity. To do so, we
rely on a name-generator task.

3.3 Study 4: Recalling Sources

So far, we've drawn conclusions about which expert sources are in journalists'
rosters based on actual news content and the expert sources journalists themselves think of when asked for their dream source. In both cases, the names
proffered were mostly men. We can surmise that this is because the networks
of sources journalists draw on are made-up of mostly men. But rather than
making this assumption, we can also ask journalists to describe a snapshot of
their source network.

Table 11 Recalled recent sources, Study 4

	First named	Second named	Third named
		Gender	
Man	72.35%	60.91%	63.89%
Woman	26.73%	37.37%	36.11%
		Race	
Black	3.70%	12.73%	22.86%
Asian	4.17%	2.73%	5.71%
Latinx	2.78%	5.45%	8.57%
White	69.00%	64.55%	51.43%
N	216	110	35

Note: At stage 1, journalists could also note if they were uncertain of a source's race. These patterns were as follows. First named: 16.67% uncertain; second named: 10.91% uncertain; third named: 8.57% uncertain.

To that end, we gave our sample of journalists a second task: a set of name-generator questions, commonly deployed in network analysis. We first asked journalists if they had ever written a story that featured an expert source. In total, 95.1% of the journalists in our sample reported that they had (at some point) written a story with an expert source. This group was then instructed to think about the last story they wrote that featured an expert source, and then prompted to provide the source's initials, their domain of expertise, their employer, gender, age, level of education, and race/ethnicity. After providing this information, journalists were next asked whether there was another expert source in that story. At this point, 53.5% reported that this was the case. Again, they were then prompted through questions that gather more information on that expert source. This process was repeated for journalists who reported having a third expert source in that same story. In total, 16.7% of journalists reported that their story had a third source.

We report the results of this task in Table 11, which presents the demographics of the expert sources. As the data show, men are more likely to be named first when journalists are asked to recall recent expert sources. They are also most likely to be be recalled second, and third.

Turning to race, the journalists report that their sources are mostly white. Indeed, among the first-named sources, 53.7% are white men. In contrast, 1.39% of first-named sources are Black women (for comparison, 2.31% are Black men).

We do not see any substantively large differences when we consider journalist gender. Although women are about 3 percentage points more likely to recall a woman as their first-named expert source, the majority of women reporters (70.21%) name men. Women are also somewhat more likely to recall a white expert source (by about 5 percentage points).[35]

In total, 46.5% of the journalists report that the source they are thinking of was someone they were contacting for the first time. This proportion varies by source gender – women are 11.2 percentage-points more likely to have been first-time sources ($p = 0.14$, two-tailed).

When we asked the journalists how they found this expert source (regardless of whether this was their first time contacting them) we see quite a bit of variance in the responses. In our question, we offered the journalists eight options (e.g., "university website," "expert database," "recommendation from another source," etc), including an "other" option where the journalists could offer their own explanation if none of the responses were suitable. Focusing on the first source, we see that 30.1% of the journalists do select this "other" option. The second most frequently selected option is "recommendation from another source" – 19.4% of the journalists select this option. This follows from research suggesting the importance of networks to sourcing (Conway, 2021).

We do see some difference in responses to this question when looking at gender of the source. Among those who listed a woman as the expert source, 25.9% reported that they found this source through a recommendation; among those who listed a man, 17.20% report that this was through a recommendation from another source. This is an 8.7 percentage point difference, but it does not meet conventional levels of statistical significance ($p = 0.16$, two-tailed). In contrast, men sources are 6.5 percentage points more likely to have been recommended to the journalist by a *colleague* (rather than another source), but again, this is difference is not statistically significant ($p = 0.26$, two-tailed).

We also see evidence that journalists are more likely to have found sources who are people of color through a recommendation from another source – something which is especially true when the source is Black. We note however, that there are very few journalists in our sample who list sources of color.

3.4 A Source of Tension?

The data in this section echo the source patterns we uncover in the *New York Times*: Journalists are more likely to name white men as (either potential or actual) sources. This is true regardless of the time they take to come up with a

---

[35] There are too few journalists of color in our sample – a reflection of the profession – to consider patterns by race.

name. The notable difference is that the journalists in our sample seem to name sources from a more diverse set of institutions, perhaps reflecting different motivations than *New York Times* reporters.

In a second task, when asked to recall their most recent expert sources, most of the journalists again list white men. We also see hints of the importance of source networks, as journalists report finding sources through recommendations from other sources. These recommendations seem especially important for women and people of color.

Overall, then the patterns in this section seems contradictory to the results presented in Section 2. In Section 2, we see that journalists prefer women and people of color as sources. How can we reconcile these two sets of results?[36]

One possibility is that the patterns in Section 2 reflect socially desirable responding, while the patterns in Sections 1 and 3 reflect actual behavior and preferences. This seems unlikely given the conjoint analysis (Bansak et al., 2021), but nonetheless social desirability may be affecting our results. Another possibility, however, is that journalists would, genuinely, prefer if their expert sources were more diverse, but face professional constraints (e.g., network limitations) in achieving this diversity. Indeed, the results in this section hint at the importance of networked recommendations from others in determining sources.

Tracking these types of professional obstacles is challenging – we could ask journalists,"How hard are you working to increase expert source diversity?" but such a question would be subject to tremendous social desirability pressures. Instead, we consider these obstacles from a different perspective. Shifting our focus from journalists' behaviors, we next look to the behavior of the expert sources themselves. In other words, we turn from investigating journalistic demand for expert sources to better understanding expert source supply.

4 Supply-Side: Expert Source Behavior

4.1 Introduction

To this point, our analyses of expert source dynamics have focused on journalists. This is an obvious population for analysis, since it is journalists who decide whom to include as expert sources in their articles (and whether to include any expert sources at all). Focusing on journalists, then, addresses the demand dynamics of expert sourcing. In this section, we shift our perspective, and

---

[36] Indeed, this disconnect between journalist preference in the abstract and journalist behavior in concrete cases has been noted in other contexts as well – for example, inclusion of children in stories (Coleman, 2011).

turn to the *supply-side* of sourcing. Rather than analyzing journalistic decision-making, we turn to a study of people who have the credentials to serve as expert sources in an article about politics – faculty in political science departments. Using this study, we consider whether there are gender and race differences in the extent to which faculty are asked to serve as expert sources. Second, we turn to a question that we could not consider with our journalist data: Are there gender and race differences in *people's experiences* once they agree to serve as expert sources? In other words, we consider the possibility journalists seek out sources to ensure source diversity, but that the experience of being an expert source is most likely to be positive for white men.

4.2 Faculty Survey

We consider expert source experiences using a survey of faculty in political science departments. To conduct the survey, we created a sample of faculty designed to represent a broad variety of academic institutions. To create this sample, we began with a population of 1,678 universities and colleges taken from the Carnegie Classification of Institutions of Higher Education. Then, each institution was classified by region and institution type. Within these geographic and institutional categories, universities were selected at random for inclusion in the sample based on their proportion within the population. We also supplemented the sample with randomly selected institutions from two groups: Historically Black colleges or universities and Ivy League institutions. Finally, we collected contact information for faculty using departmental websites. We include additional information about sample construction in Online Appendix D.1.

We contacted faculty in two waves. An initial set of 889 faculty were contacted in February 2021, yielding 163 responses, for a response rate of 17.3%. We supplemented this initial sample with an additional set of institutions, and contacted 673 additional faculty in July 2021. This second round of contact yielded 150 responses, for a response rate of 21.9%.[37] In Online Appendix D.2, we consider any potential selection effects in the types of faculty members who completed the survey, and find little evidence to this point. We present the demographics of our sample – separating the February and July rounds – in Table 12. All reported demographics in Table 12 are based on self-identification in the survey. All survey questions are reported in Online Appendix D.3.

---

[37] Response rates calculated using AAPOR RR1.

Table 12 Sample characteristics, faculty study

	Full sample	Feb wave	July wave
Gender			
Men	64.56%	62.50%	74.51%
Women	34.74%	36.88%	24.51%
Race			
Asian	4.78%	5.16%	3.96%
Black	4.41%	4.52%	4.95%
Latinx	5.15%	5.81%	4.95%
White	81.99%	83.23%	81.19%
Subfield			
American	50.7%	53.16%	51.96%
Comparative	15.14%	16.46%	12.75%
IR	17.96%	19.62%	17.65%
Methods	1.06%	1.27%	0.98%
Theory	6.69%	3.80%	6.86%
Years since degree			
Fewer than 5 years	10.18%	8.75%	6.86%
5–10 years	19.65%	18.75%	18.63%
11–20 years	35.09%	35.62%	37.25%
More than 21 years	35.09%	36.88%	37.25%
Institution type			
Public	47.45%	43.95%	48.51%
Private	33.58%	38.22%	29.70%
Liberal Arts college	17.88%	16.56%	21.78%

The faculty in our sample were invited to complete a survey via the email addresses listed on their institutional websites. The invitation described the survey as a study of "interactions between media professionals and scholars." In the February 2021 round of contact, the invitation further noted that we were "interested in [their] experiences with media interview requests." We believe that this line may have discouraged those who had no media experiences from participating. Therefore, in the July 2021 round, we edited that line in the invitation to read, "We are interested in your responses whether you speak with media or do not speak with media." It is possible that this edit produced the somewhat higher response rate in the July 2021 round.

It is important to acknowledge, however, that this invitation may have produced a notable limitation in our survey: faculty who had never received any media requests may have been less likely to take the survey, thinking that they would not have anything to offer on the topic. Indeed, in our survey, only 4.61% of respondents say that they have never had a media request; 2.78% say this is the case in the February round, and 6.52% report no media requests in the July round. It is certainly possible that 95% of political science faculty have received a media request at least once in their careers. Still, the increase in the proportion of faculty without a media request in the July round does hint at the possibility that our invitation affected the types of respondents who participated.

Being cognizant of this limitation, we do *not* use our survey to consider the likelihood of receiving media requests. Rather, we use our survey to track variation in the experiences of faculty who have received media requests.

We also want to underscore an important demographic limitation in our survey: Given our overall sample size, the number of faculty in our survey who identify as people of color is small (30 in total). To some extent, our survey reflects political science as a discipline. According to APSA, for example, 4.5% of APSA members are Black; in our survey, 4.41% of respondents report that they are Black. At the same time, we do want to draw attention to the racial differences in our results – particularly when it comes to faculty experiences as a result of appearing as an expert source. We report these differences in the text, but we want to note the small sample, which does not allow us to disaggregate our results further (e.g., intersection of race and gender). This is a critical limitation.

4.3 Media Requests

We begin by considering two basic ideas. First, do rates of requests vary by faculty characteristics. Here, we first consider whether faculty gender and race affect request frequency. Beyond the rate of media requests, we also consider the experience of receiving a media request. In this section, we first focus on the extent to which there are demographic differences in who is recommended as an expert source to journalists. Then, we consider the basic logistics of the request: the mode and the time offered for response. Given our findings in Section 1, we also analyze the role of institution type. We find few clear differences either by institution type or departmental rank. However, following the patterns we see in Sections 1 and 3, we find that full professors are most likely to receive media contact.

4.3.1 Rate of Requests

As a first step, we compare self-reported patterns of media requests among those respondents who report having any media requests.[38] Here, we use two separate measures – one to capture media requests during election years and the other to capture requests during off-years. This is to account for the possibility that there are more stories that necessitate political science expertise during election years. All participants were told that to answer the question, they should think of "requests made by journalists from professional media outlets **(not student media outlets)** [bold in the original]."

We present our results in Figure 5. First, we note that the gender differences in rates of media requests are not statistically significant. We find that neither the means nor the distributions – in both the election and non-election measures – differ significantly by gender.[39] In other words, men and women report statistically similar rates of media requests. We note, however, men are 9.98 percentage points more likely to report that they receive frequent media requests (i.e., several times per week) during election periods (p=0.023, two-tailed).[40]

Figure 5 focuses on gender differences in rates of media requests; the results show that faculty of color and white faculty report receiving media requests at similar rates.

Differences by Professional Rank When we consider source patterns in previous sections, we see patterns by the gender and race of scholars. We also see another pattern: Expert sources are most likely to be full professors. In Section 1, for example, 56.43% of all political experts in our *New York Times* sample were full professors, and among political experts interviewed more than once, 83.33% were full professors (see Table 3). In Section 3, about 70% of all academics listed as "ideal sources" on a political topic were full professors (see Table 10). Therefore, we use our faculty survey to consider whether faculty professional rank affects patterns of requests. We present our results in Table 13. We find that while full professors do seem to receive more frequent media contact, the group differences in Table 13 are not significant.

---

[38] The 4.61% of respondents who reported no media requests at all were not asked these questions.

[39] Mean comparisons: Election-time: $t = -1.2214$, p = 0.223; Non-election time: $t = -0.6568$, $p = 0.511$, both two-tailed. Distribution comparisons, Kolmogorov–Smirnov Tests: Election-time: $D = 0.0998, p = 0.630$; Non-election-time: $D = 0.0975, p = 0.646$. We do not see any differences in reported frequency of media contact by survey round.

[40] We find similar patterns if we limit our analysis only to faculty who specify that their research interests are in elections and voting behavior, though we note that limits our respondents to $N = 68$.

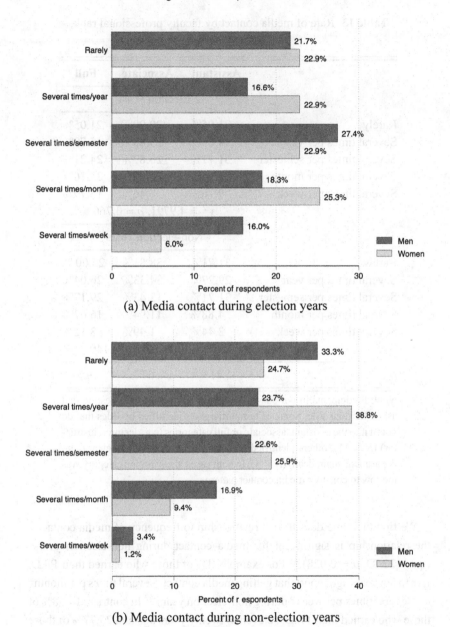

(a) Media contact during election years

(b) Media contact during non-election years

Figure 5 Political science faculty media requests, faculty study

It is possible, however, that what we see as a rank effect in previous sections is more of a *time* effect – perhaps full professors are more likely to be sources not due to their titles, but to the fact that they have simply been in their jobs longer. The benefit of the faculty survey is that, in addition to ranks, we also asked our participants how long ago they earned their Ph.D.s.

Table 13 Rate of media contact by faculty professional rank,
faculty study

	Assistant	Associate	Full
	Election years		
Rarely	21.95%	20.90%	21.05%
Several times per year	14.63%	23.88%	15.79%
Several times per semester	31.71%	26.87%	24.21%
Several times per month	21.95%	20.90%	23.16%
Several times per week	9.76%	7.46%	15.79%
	$\chi^2 = 4.9791, p = 0.760$		
	Non-election years		
Rarely	31.71%	38.81%	25.00 %
Several times per year	29.27%	34.33%	26.04%
Several times per semester	31.71%	13.43%	29.17%
Several times per month	4.88%	11.94%	16.67%
Several times per week	2.44%	1.49%	3.12%
	$\chi^2 = 12.0510, p = 0.149$		
N	41	67	95

Note: Participants in our survey answered an open-ended question that
asked for their title. Some of our participants identified by titles that do
not fit into the assistant, associate or full categories (e.g., lecturer, instruc-
tor) ($N = 11$); others identified by titles where rank was not clear (e.g.,
department chair, dean) ($N = 4$). In both cases, the N for the category was
too low to consider media contact patterns.

We find that time does have a relationship to frequency of media contact –
the relationship is significant for media contact during non-election years
($\chi^2 = 22.93, p = 0.028$).[41] For example, 4% of those who earned their Ph.D.
five to ten years ago report that getting media contact "several times per month"
or "several times per week" during non-election years.[42] In contrast, 14.58% of
those who earned their Ph.D.s eleven to twenty years ago and 25.77% of those
who earned their Ph.D.s more than twenty-one years ago report this level of
media contact during non-election years. Although those who have had their
Ph.D.s longer are more likely to be contacted during election years as well, the

---

[41] For election-time patterns: $\chi^2 = 13.8055, p = 0.313$.
[42] No faculty in this group report getting contact "several times per week" during non-election
years – so the 4% is solely from the per-month category.

patterns are more muted and the rate of contact hovers around 30% for all the groups.[43]

These patterns, then, suggest a possibility that rank may be a proxy for time. In other words, journalists are not deliberately seeking out full professors because they have achieved the rank, but because the rank is a reflection of time spent in academia. Time in itself, of course, may be a proxy for other factors that affect media contact. More time in academia means more time to establish contacts – with other academics and with journalists and, potentially, media relations staff within one's own institution. Time since Ph.D. is also reflective of age and may hint at the idea that journalists are more comfortable approaching older expert sources. We cannot adjudicate between these explanations using our data – and it is also difficult to pinpoint precisely why these patterns emerge most clearly during non-election years. Still, we would speculate that all of these different time-related factors intersect to increase the presence of "older" faculty as expert sources. Since journalists need more political experts during election years, they end up reaching out to wider groups; when there is no election, the stories – and the expert sources – may be more limited.

Differences by Institution Type Although our focus in this section has been on the role of gender and race in faculty experiences with journalists, we do want to consider whether institution type affects the patterns of requests we see among our faculty sample. This follows from our results in Section 1, which suggest that expert sources in the *New York Times* were more likely to come from research institutions – as well as previous research suggesting expert sources were more likely to have affiliations with Ivy League schools (e.g., Soley, 1992).

We first present our results by institution type in Table 14. Overall, we see few consistent differences. Faculty at private institutions are somewhat more likely to report being contacted "several times per week" during election times. In contrast, faculty at Liberal Arts colleges are more likely to fall into this category during non-election periods, though the number of faculty from this group in our sample is small. Still, there are few clear patterns in these results.

Taking a different approach, in Table 15 we consider media requests by the rank of the faculty member's employing department. We split the rank at 30, as 50.96% of our respondents work at departments ranked 1-30. The third column

---

[43] Proportion of group reporting media contact "several times per month" or "several times per week" during elections, by time from Ph.D.: 5 years or fewer – 28.58%; 5–10 years – 29.16%; 11–20 years – 31.58%; 21+ years –37.5%.

Table 14 Rate of media contact by institution type, faculty study

	Public	Private	LAC
	Election years		
Rarely	26.05%	19.10%	18.75%
Several times per year	16.81%	16.85%	22.92%
Several times per semester	30.25%	21.35%	27.08%
Several times per month	15.97%	25.84%	20.83%
Several times per week	10.92%	16.85%	10.42%
	$\chi^2 = 7.89, p = 0.445$		
	Non-election years		
Rarely	36.13%	23.33%	31.25%
Several times per year	25.21%	27.78%	33.33%
Several times per semester	27.73%	21.11%	22.92%
Several times per month	8.40%	23.33%	0
Several times per week	2.52%	4.44%	12.50%
	$\chi^2 = 14.92, p = 0.061$		
N	119	89	48

Note: Participants were asked to select their institution type. In addition to those listed in this table, three participants reported that they work at an HBCU.

is for faculty respondents who do not work at Ph.D.-granting departments, which means that their departments are not ranked.[44]

Here, we do see some differences, although they are between those at Ph.D-granting and non-Ph.D.-granting departments. Those at non-Ph.D.-granting departments do report receiving fewer media requests – but the patterns are only significant during non-election years. We do not see any clear, consistent differences by rank, however. While this may be an artifact of our ranking split, it echoes what we saw in our Section 1 content analysis, where we also saw no clear differences by departmental rank.[45]

---

[44] The ranks were self-reported by the survey participants.

[45] We conducted a similar analysis using the rank of the department where the survey participants earned their Ph.D. and find no clear differences in media contact by rank (again split between 1–30 and 30+ as 58.08% of our participants earned their Ph.D. at an institution ranked 1–30). We see no significant patterns for either election time contact ($\chi^2 = 0.96, p = 0.916$) or non-election time contact ($\chi^2 = 5.81, p = 0.214$).

Table 15 Rate of media contact by departmental rank, faculty study

	1–30	31+	Non-Ph.D.
	Election Years		
Rarely	17.65%	18.75%	26.36%
Several times per year	15.69%	16.67%	18.18%
Several times per semester	27.45%	27.08%	26.36%
Several times per month	23.53%	20.83%	18.18%
Several times per week	15.69%	16.67%	10.91%
	$\chi^2 = 3.32, p = 0.913$		
	Non-election years		
Rarely	15.38%	27.08%	38.18%
Several times per year	28.85%	18.75%	30.00%
Several times per semester	25.00%	31.25%	21.82%
Several times per month	25.00%	18.75%	8.18%
Several times per week	5.77%	4.17%	1.82%
	$\chi^2 = 18.35, p = 0.019$		
N	51	48	110

4.3.2 Recommendations

Thus far, we find few differences in rates of requests, though we do find that the faculty who report receiving media requests "several times per week" are more likely to be men who are full professors. As a next step, then, we turn to people's experiences. We begin by considering how faculty may come to receive a media request by way of a peer's recommendation.

We find that most of the faculty in our survey (81.13%) reported having received media requests because someone had recommended them to a journalist. The rate was nearly identical for both men (80.9%) and women (81.18%). We also see similar rates of reported recommendation rates among faculty of color (78.85%) and white faculty (81.69%).These results lend support to patterns we uncovered in Section 1, which suggest network connections among sources may in part explain expert source patterns.

4.3.3 Contact Logistics

Another consideration is *how* journalists contact the faculty in our sample. One simple comparison is the mode of contact: email, telephone, or social media. Unsurprisingly, most contact is conducted via email; in total, 75.09% report that journalists "typically" contact them via email. Less expected, however, is that there is gender difference in mode of contact: men are less likely to be contacted by email ($p < 0.011$, two-tailed). Certainly, a majority of men still report contact via email, but we do see a 14.5 percentage point difference between men and women. We see no differences in mode of contact by race.

We asked our participants to estimate "On average, how many days turn-around do journalists give you for media requests?" The plurality of our participants, 41.22%, report that the average length of time to respond is one day. We do, however, find small, but notable, gender differences. While 43.2% of men report that journalists often give them a turnaround of "several hours" to respond, only 29.8% of women selected that option.[46] In other words, men seem to get less time for response.

Notably, for men there is also a relationship between the turnaround time journalists offer and the frequency of media requests. Men who report short turnaround times are also significantly more likely to have had more inter-views, both during election times and otherwise; this is not the case for women.[47]

Taken together, the ways that men in our sample experience media requests relative to women – contact via the phone, less turnaround time, and less time accompanying more frequent requests – suggest that the nature of the rela-tionship between source and journalist in these instances, with men experts, may be different. It may be the case that journalists, short on time, are return-ing to the same set of sources, sources which are more likely to be men. It is also not outside the realm of possibility that these differences in contact speak to longer-term relationships between journalist and source, which are more likely to be present for men. Indeed, in her article examining the diver-sity of sources in her work over the course of a year, *The Atlantic* reporter Adrienne LaFrance found that men experts were more likely to be sourced for multiple articles, while she did not return to a single woman expert (LaFrance, 2016). She cites time pressures as one reason for this gender imbalance, but also explains that of the various topical areas she covers, men are more likely to be at the top of the call sheet, and thus, returned to over and over again for comment. Her personal experience echoes what we find in our data, from

---

[46] The options were as follow: (a) several hours, (b) 1 day, (c) 2 days, (d) 3 days, (e) 4 or more days. A Kolmogorov–Smirnov test shows that there is not a significant distributional difference by gender when we consider all the categories, $p = 0.257$.

[47] Among men, those who report shorter turnaround time report more frequent media requests during elections, $p = 0.004$, and during non-election times, $p = 0.015$. Among women, those who report shorter turnaround times report *fewer* media requests during elections ($p = 0.0428$) and *fewer* requests during non-election times (0.562).

the angle of both journalistic demand and expert supply, we find a reoccurring theme: characteristics of expert networks ultimately affect *who* makes it to the news.

4.3.4 Who Is Asked?

Generally, then, we find that among people who have received a media request, men and women self-report receiving these requests at similar rates. Given the gender disparities among political science faculty, however, this general equivalence in media requests may translate to the types of gender disparities we observe in our *New York Times* data. APSA reports that, as of 2020, 37.5% of its members are women (which includes non-faculty members; for example, graduate students). In our survey, 34.98% of the respondents are women. Given existing disciplinary gender disparities, if men and women receive interview requests at equivalent rates, news outlets will mimic this very same gender distribution. Moreover, if media requests shift – even slightly – to favor men (as our election-time measure suggests), then this gender imbalance will likely be further exacerbated.

The same, of course, can be said of race – except the disparities among political scientists are even more stark. Contacting faculty of color at the same rate as white faculty again translates the disparities of academic departments to expert sources in news articles. Not only that, but if the relationship between requested turnaround time from journalists and frequency of requests signals some greater connection between journalist and source, then this connection is much more present for white men.[48]

4.4 Declining Requests

As next step, we consider faculty responses to media requests. Here, we first ask our participants how often they accept the media requests they receive. What emerges from the faculty data is that men *accept* interview requests at higher rates than women. Among men, 49.7% of respondents report that they accept media requests either "always" or "almost always." Among women, 33.7% report doing the same. On average, men are significantly more likely to accept interview requests with greater frequency ($p = 0.006$, two-tailed).[49] If men and women are asked to serve as expert sources at relatively equal rates (and possibly, men are asked at higher rates during elections), but men are more likely

---

[48] Indeed, among white men who report being given short turnaround times, nearly 20% report getting media requests several times per week.

[49] We note that when we compare distributions using a Kolmogorov–Smirnov test, the results fall short of significance: $D = 0.16, p = 0.102$.

to accept interview requests, then jointly these two patterns, again, exacerbate already-existing gender disparities among political science scholars.

These patterns, however, lead to a question: Why are women accepting interview requests at lower rates than men? To track why scholars decline media requests, we asked participants to select from a series of reasons for declining; the options included "I don't have time," "I don't feel comfortable with the topic," "Fear of repercussions or harassment," or, simply "I don't like interviews." In total, there were fourteen different options for declining and participants could select as many reasons as they wanted.[50] We present the results, by gender, in Table 16, where we find, generally, few gender differences in reasons for declining – with one exception. The results in Table 16 are also robust to a Benjamini-Hochberg correction for multiple comparisons.

The modal reason for declining interviews is discomfort with the topic of interview. Here we see that both men and women are highly likely to offer this as a reason, although men are 9.6 percentage points more likely to select this reason.

The next set of commonly selected reasons are focused on time. Research suggests that women in academia often take on more invisible labor within departments (Reid, 2021), which could suggest that women may be more likely to decline interviews because they simply do not have the time. In our data, however, similar proportions of men and women report that they decline interviews due to time constraints. And, where we do see gender differences – "scheduling difficulties" – it is because a higher percentage of men select that reason.[51]

Where we see the most pronounced gender difference is in the proportions of individuals who select "fear of repercussions or harassment" as a reason for declining interviews. Although a minority of our sample selected this as a reason, women were more likely to do so – a difference of 11 percentage points.

Ultimately, these results suggest that when scholars decline interviews it is most often due to topic or time, but for women there may be additional concerns about harassment.

4.4.1 Results: Media Experiences

As a final step, we consider differences in people's experiences with journalists. Here, we also analyze *post-interview* experiences, tracking the extent to

---

[50] There was also an "Other" option where participants could offer a specific reason; 10.2% of participants selected this option.

[51] A difference of 9.2 percentage points.

Table 16 Percent selecting reason for declining media requests, faculty study

	Men	Women	Difference	*p*-value
	Time			
Don't have time	48.04%	51.19%	3.15	0.64
Turnaround too tight	26.73%	37.37%	−1.49	0.82
Scheduling is difficult	31.84%	22.62%	−9.22	0.12
	Journalist/Outlet			
Interview mode	7.26%	8.33%	1.07	0.76
Outlet not prestigious	6.15%	10.71%	4.56	0.19
Don't know the journalist	7.82%	4.76%	−3.06	0.36
	Discomfort			
Uncomfortable with topic	71.5%	61.9%	−9.6	0.12
Dislike interviews	10.61%	11.9%	1.29	0.76
	Negative Outcomes			
Fear of harassment	4.47%	15.48%	11.01	0.002
Prior negative experience	5.03%	11.01%	5.98	0.93
	Institution			
Institution doesn't value	7.26%	4.76%	−2.5	0.44
Institution discourages	1.19%	1.68%	0.49	0.76
N	179	87		

which people receive negative feedback or harassment from the public after appearing as experts in news stories. In particular, we consider whether there are differences in experiences that could discourage future participation. We present our results in Table 17.

We begin with a question of credit: How often have the faculty in our sample provided information to a journalist, but were given no credit for doing so in the final article? Here we find that men are more likely to have had this experience. In our sample, 41.4% of men report that this has happened to them "a number of times," compared to 20.2% of women who selected the same response.

Next, we consider feedback: How often have members of the public provided unsolicited feedback on media appearances? We find few differences by gender. Women are slightly more likely to have received any feedback

Table 17 Experiences post-media appearance, faculty study

	Men	Women	Difference
	Received no credit		
Never	35.63%%	44.05%	8.42
Has happened	22.99%	35.71%	12.72
Happened often	41.38%	20.24%	−21.14
Difference:	Distribution: $p = 0.013$		
	Mean: $p = 0.009$		
	Unsolicited feedback from public		
Never	41.24%	39.53%	−1.71
Mostly positive feedback	27.12%	29.07%	1.95
Mostly Negative Feedback	3.39%	5.81%	2.42
Mixed Feedback	28.25%	25.58%	−2.67
Difference:	Distribution: $p = 1.00$		
	Mean: $p = 0.664$		
	Received threats after appearance		
Never	15.08%	17.44%	2.36
Has Happened	84.92%	82.56%	−2.36
Difference:	Distribution: $p = 1.00$		
	Mean: $p = 0.624$		
N	179	87	

post–media appearance, but the difference is substantively very small, 1.71 percentage points. We also do not see evidence that the feedback women receive is more negative, rather women are more likely to have received both positive and negative feedback.

As a next step, we look at a more dangerous outcome: harassment. Specifically, we ask participants whether they have ever been threatened by someone (in any capacity) following a media appearance. In total, 16.04% of the participants report that they have been threatened. We also see small differences between men and women: women are 2.36 percentage points more likely to report receiving threats.

Overall, then, we see few gender differences in people's experiences after giving a media interview, and where these differences exist, they are small. Keeping the limitations of our data in mind, we do, however, want to consider patterns by race – where we find more notable differences.

First, faculty who identify as people of color are 10.8 percentage points more likely than white faculty to receive unsolicited feedback after a media appearance. Moreover, they are also 7.4 percentage points more likely than white faculty to receive feedback that is negative or mixed.

There are also considerable differences in levels of harassment; faculty of color are 8.78 percentage points more likely to report having been threatened after a media appearance. Indeed, nearly a quarter of faculty of color in our survey who do media interviews also report experiencing threats. In short, we see that faculty of color are more likely to have had negative – and threatening – experiences when they agree to act as expert sources.

4.5 Expert Experiences versus Journalistic Preferences

The results of the faculty survey add still another complication to the patterns we show in this Element. First, we see evidence that there are few demographic differences in media requests overall. At the same time, we do see that people who get nearly weekly requests are more likely to be men. We also see hints of relationships between these frequent sources and journalists, for example, in the fact that these same sources are more likely to receive less time to respond.

How do we reconcile the patterns we see in the faculty survey with the patterns we see in the *New York Times* data (Section 1) and the patterns we see in our four studies of journalists (Sections 2 and 3)? Altogether, the data point to a nuanced pattern. Women and people of color are underrepresented as expert sources about politics. In the abstract, journalists report that they would like to interview more diverse expert sources. Yet, as we show in this section, these goals in the *abstract* may not translate to actual diversity in expert sources.

Given that there are many more white, men on faculty in political science departments, in order to increase the presence of women and people of color as expert sources, journalists would need to contact them at higher rates. This is not what we find in our faculty survey. Rather, because rates of contact are similar across groups, the disparities in political science itself translate to disparities in political news stories.

5 Constructing Political Expertise

As we were finishing this Element, the *New York Times* published the special series "The Root of Haiti's Misery: Reparations to Enslavers" (Porter et al., 2022a). The series detailed the "suffocating debts that France and later the United States imposed on Haiti after its independence"; the series was as the *New York Times* itself noted, "built on more than a century of scholarship. Many historians, economists and others who have studied these issues were quoted directly in the articles" (*New York Times*, 2022). The series came with a separate GitHub page of data and a bibliography of sources used for the report (Porter et al., 2022b).

Along with this report, though, came criticisms from historians: "I spoke with [Catherine Porter] at length when she was first embarking on this research," tweeted historian Mary Lewis. "I told her about my sources, I connected her with my research assistant in France. She presumably contacted me b/c [sic] she'd read my work. No acknowledgement"(Shafer, 2022).[52] Other historians responded to Lewis' story on Twitter, sharing that they had similar experiences. Still others noted that "the paper presented the roots of Haiti's present-day poverty as a mystery that its reporters had just solved, without giving sufficient credit to the many historians, many of them people of color, who've been researching the topic for years" (Allsop, 2022).

How journalists use the work of historians is a complicated question (e.g., McGuire, 2018), but we can also bring it back to the case at hand: *Whose* names get included in a story as an expert source is important. More than just a news decision, journalists' selection of expert sources constructs expertise – and this construction has consequences. For experts, the construction of expertise can affect opportunities for external funding, perceptions of research agenda legitimacy, and entry into public discourse. Perhaps most importantly, sourcing decisions affect *who* gets elevated as an expert in a given domain, and, which *ideas* become dominant.

In this Element we consider *who* gets to be a political expert in the news. We start in Section 1 by conducting a content analysis on 2020 U.S. election coverage in the *New York Times*, an analysis which yielded a portrait of who gets to be a political expert in this domain: white men, full professors at R1 universities, with larger than average Twitter followings. Of course, analyzing sources at the *New York Times* cannot tell us everything, but it can gives us some indication of who is on the roster of expert sources for major legacy outlets, which set the agenda for other news outlets. Since we also find that journalists often return to the same political experts multiple times, the data suggest that *some* have more opportunities than others to communicate science. Scholar and journalist networks, the patterns in Section 1 hint, can be "sticky."

To understand who makes the cut, we next try to uncover what drives the decisions of those who make the expert source rosters: journalists. In Section 2 we find that, in contrast to what one might expect given the patterns of political expertise on the pages of the *New York Times*, when given the choice between several research vignettes, journalists find women researchers to be

---

[52] Lewis' tweet used *New York Times* reporter Catherine Porter's Twitter handle.

more newsworthy than their peers. To tease apart this puzzling pattern, we rely on a conjoint experiment, which allows us to compare source characteristics beyond gender. This approach permits more precision in determining which characteristics of expert sources matter most, but also allows us to get around the possibility that journalists are giving us socially desirable, rather than genuine, responses regarding what and who they perceive to be deserving of news coverage (Bansak et al., 2021).

First and foremost, this analysis suggests that – all things being equal – journalists *prefer* women and non-white expert sources. Given that one of the purposes of such analyses is to reveal true preferences, juxtaposed against the cast of mostly white men expert sources presented in Section 1, this result is surprising. We also uncovered a preference for experts from *any* institution type (except community colleges), with high citation counts, moderate Twitter followings, and local media experience.

Perhaps, however, these journalist preferences emerge due to the abstractions in the experimental designs in Section 2. In Section 3, we move away from more abstract journalistic decisions, asking journalists to tell us more about who they source. In the first experiment, we mimic newsroom constraints by asking some journalists to tell us who their ideal political expert source is under experimentally imposed time pressure. We find that, regardless of whether their decision was timed or not, journalists report a preference for academic men. Like in the *New York Times* data, we also see a preference for full professors. However, unlike that same data, there is no significant preference for academics from research universities. This is likely the result of differences between journalists in the sample, and *New York Times* journalists. We also ask journalists to engage in a name-generator task that helps us to understand characteristics of their source networks. This task, again, suggests that journalists have source networks made-up of mostly men, and mostly white experts.

In Section 4, we survey the potential universe for those expert source networks – political science faculty in the United States – in an attempt to understand how supply-side behaviors might play a role. We find that women and men report receiving interview requests at similar rates, however, women report turning down such requests more often than their colleagues. Why is this the case? Women report more fear of being harassed, although the rate of reported harassment by both men and women is the same. This gap between the possibility for, and actual harassment of women experts in our sample, offers one explanation. Showing a similar pattern, potential women political candidates are more likely to be aware of online harassment, and this shapes their perceptions of hostile working environments (Wagner, 2020). Notably, the volume of harassment reported by faculty of color as a result of media requests is higher than among white faculty. This is in line with previous studies. Surveys show that people of color face more severe online harassment (Vogels, 2021). Moreover, research also demonstrates that Black Twitter users are especially concerned about journalists embedding their tweets in news stories because it leads to harassment; this is especially true for Black women (Freelon et al., 2018).

The patterns in Section 4 also return to another pattern we saw in Section 1. When we consider the logistics of this contact, we see that there are certain scholars who receive more media contact and who are given less time to respond, suggestive of the idea that journalists are more likely to have relationships with certain scholars, and return to those scholars for quick expert comment turnaround. This, we suggest, is symptomatic of two interconnected ideas. First, as we suggest in Section 1, journalists develop a list of experts to whom they return over and over again. Second, the experts on this list are more likely to be white men.

These patterns, as we suggest in Section 1, speak to a set of multilevel influences in news production (Reese & Shoemaker, 2016; Shoemaker & Reese, 2014). Micro-level, individual preferences intersect with organizational constraints, which are further shaped by broader institutional structures of academia. The patterns we observe are a function of multiple forces, shaping the choice architectures journalists and academic experts work within.

5.1 Why These Experts?

So where does this leave us? A few things are evident. First, from a methodological perspective, we need more data and increased use of experimental methods to better understand which types of people are more likely to be expert sources. Without a multisample, multimethod approach we would have ended up with a very different understanding of political expertise in news. But the question of who is included in the news requires a still broader approach. Mellado and Scherman (2021) find, for example, source diversity varies by platform. Moreover, as Merkley (2020) suggests, the way journalists frame expert opinions – and the other sources cited alongside the experts – may also shape the construction of expertise.

Second, when we observe political expertise in the news, and when we survey and talk to journalists, it becomes clear that the expert pictures in our heads do not necessarily reveal *journalistic preference* for who makes up those pictures. Given hypotheticals, journalists reveal a preference for non-white, women expert sources. When recounting real world expert source decisions, however, journalists tend to select white men. In this context, the decision calculus amounts to this: a preference for non-white and women experts does not equate to more diverse sources, *actually seeking out more diverse experts leads to more diverse sources.*

This also matches up with *The Atlantic* journalist Ed Yong's anecdotal evidence that diversifying his own expert source pool effectively required him to oversample women. Detailing his goal to increase the number of women experts included in his stories, Yong found that he "would need to contact around 1.3 men to get one male quote, and around 1.6 women to get one women one"(Yong, 2018). Yong noted that searching for these additional voices adds "15 minutes per piece, or an hour or so of effort over a week. That seems like a trifling amount, and the bare minimum that journalists should strive for." He has also since began actively working to increase the number of people of color who appear as expert sources in his articles. "I knew that I care about equality, so I deluded myself into thinking that I wasn't part of the problem," Yong wrote. "I assumed that my passive concern would be enough. Passive concern never is."[53]

It is also important to situate representation of expert sources not only as who is represented but *how often* these people are represented. There is some evidence in our data to suggest that networks of journalists and expert sources are "sticky." Writing about representation in her own stories, Adrienne LaFrance distinguishes between "one-off" stories" that include experts she does not anticipate interviewing again, and experts who appear consistently in her "dedicated beats" (LaFrance, 2016).

These "sticky" networks, we suggest, underscore what we observe in our data. First, as LaFrance (2016) writes, experts who happen to make it to "the first person on [a journalist's] to-call list" (to use LaFrance's words) are more likely to be white men. Our data imply the same patterns. In Section 3, for example, when journalists are asked to think of a political expert source who comes to mind, they are most likely to think of white men.

The possibility of these "sticky" networks and "to-call lists," however, also suggest another idea that our data do not capture. It is possible that as journalists return to experts repeatedly, certain scholarly ideas are also consistently more likely to make the news even in areas where there is a good deal of scholarly debate.

---

[53] *New York Times* writer David Leonhardt (2018) came to a similar conclusion that his work was not including enough women as sources. Both Yong and Leonhardt credit Adrienne LaFrance with raising the issue of gender balance in the news. Writing in 2013, LaFrance ended her piece with: "Let everyone else interview Larry Sabato ... for the zillionth time" (LaFrance, 2013). It is worth noting, that in our survey of journalists, Sabato was the most mentioned expert source.

Imagine, for example, that there is a long-standing scholarly discussion in academic journals and at conferences about the relationship between some variable X and some other variable Y. How we characterize the relationship, research suggests, may depend on measurement and method. How X and Y are presented in the news, however, may depend on which scholar serves as an expert source. And, if journalists return to the same expert consistently, then the public image of X and Y will depend heavily on that scholar's particular perspective of an academic debate. Hence, the public will observe an apparent expert consensus regarding this topic when the reality is that the experts do not agree.

Even more broadly, the possibility that journalists return to the same experts consistently serve as an important context for calls for a more public-facing science (e.g., Dudo & Besley, 2016). When calls are made for academics to be effective at communicating their research or for more women and experts of color to do public-facing work, they are often done under the assumption that the playing field is equal. Our data suggests that that is not the case. In other words, if no journalists decide that an academic is an expert worth including in the news, it does not matter if an academic is media trained. And, as our data hint, remaining in the list of possible expert sources seems easier than breaking into that list (see Ossa, 2022 for a discussion of which experts and, even more broadly, which *universities* make the news).

5.2 The Future Expert Source Landscape?

Characterizing why some people are more likely to end up as expert sources, however, is not the same as suggesting how or if this list of sources could ever grow broader. We will not claim to provide the magic solution in this Element. Rather, we suggest some points to consider when seeking source diversity.

First, it is important to think of source selection as a multilayer issue rather than a decision made by an individual journalist (e.g Reese & Shoemaker, 2016). Our data show a tension between journalist preferences under ideal scenarios and their behaviors under institutional constraints – a complicated pattern that echoes what both LaFrance (2016) and Yong (2018) found in their own sourcing. Blaming journalists without an understanding of the unique institutional contexts within which they operate, then, is counterproductive.

From this perspective, newsroom efforts to increase the diversity of sources in the news should also look beyond a focus only on journalists. If newsrooms are serious about broadening their pools of sources they must support journalists by giving them the time, resources, and space to do so. More broadly, these types of efforts could be part of broader educational initiatives about inclusion

(Geertsema-Sligh et al., 2020). Within this context, although recent efforts to bring more diversity, equity, and inclusion initiatives (DEI) to newsrooms are important, they may not (on their own) be sufficient when it comes to sourcing. In interviews with journalists and managers spearheading DEI efforts within newsrooms, Brown (2020) finds a gap between newsroom promises and the resources and commitment required to fulfill such promises.

The focus on source diversity as a "journalist decision-making" issue, however, also means that there is less attention to the dynamics of expert communities – in our case, academic political scientists. That journalists are doubtlessly key gatekeepers in whose expertise is elevated does not mean that all experts begin at an equal distance from the gate. Certainly, differences in institutional prestige affect whose voices make the news – the "golden rolodex" Soley (1992). This may be in part, as Ossa (2022) suggests, due to networks: "Why do media outlets tend to work so frequently with professors from elite schools? Perhaps because they employ editors who went to those schools," Ossa writes.

But the power of institutional prestige may work beyond networks. Academic institutions have media offices, with the goal of "investing in PR in order to provide media visibility and raise stakeholder acceptance"(Marcinkowski et al., 2014, 62). Within these offices, "academic knowledge has been customized in journalistic form in anticipation of its use in the media" (Rowe & Brass, 2008, 693). This packaging, then, may increase the inclusion of academic research – and the researcher as an expert – in the news (Rowe & Brass, 2008). Indeed, there is evidence to suggest that press releases not only increase the coverage of science, but that the resulting articles even included verbatim passages from the press releases (Comfort et al., 2022). Given the time constraints journalists face, university press releases may prove pivotal (Autzen, 2014).

It is possible, then, that university media offices could help journalists diversify sources by introducing them to new political knowledge and facilitating connections to new researchers. Yet the capabilities of these offices likely differ across universities. Some media offices likely have more funding and staff than others – and these resources likely correlate with the resources of the universities themselves. Institutional prestige likely also influences the reach of the press releases produced by these offices. Moreover, there is also important variance in the relationships between researchers and university media offices. While Marcinkowski et al. (2014) find, for example, that STEM faculty (rather than social science or humanities) have closer relationships with university PR, it is possible that relationships develop between individual faculty members and media office staff (much as they do between individual faculty members and journalists). Presumably, those academics with closer ties are more likely to have their research packaged by the media office.

Ultimately, then, it is possible that university media offices may actually exacerbate issues of institutional prestige and "sticky networks" in sources. Some academics are more likely to get the attention of their media office, and some institutions have media offices that are better resourced and more prominent. Indeed, while journalists' organizational context is important to understanding sourcing, the organizational context within universities is likely also a pivotal part of the story. Journalists are often encouraged to audit their sources, and it is likely that university media offices may benefit from a similar audit of the researchers whose work they package.[54]

It is also important to acknowledge the differences in people's experiences as expert sources. Increasingly, both sources *and* journalists are targets for online harassment, and women and people of color are more likely to be singled out (Posetti et al., 2021). Indeed, our faculty survey data (Section 4) show evidence to this point. To the extent that being public-facing is important to some institutions – for example, 34.3% of respondents in our faculty survey reported that media requests are included in their annual evaluations – these institutions would do well to consider how they may protect faculty from online abuse and harassment.[55] Advocacy efforts to encourage more diverse public-facing scholarship that do not pay attention to the potential for harm resultant from this public-facing work are incomplete. Indeed, recent studies from UNESCO and the International Center for Journalists (Posetti & Shabbir, 2022) make clear that institutions need to actively protect journalists. If we value diversity in the newsroom as well as diversity in the news, institutions – newsrooms and universities alike – need to take appropriate security and harm reduction measures.

In the end then, there is no simple answer for increasing source diversity. Of course, a large part of the effort falls to journalists, but it would be a mistake to suggest that who makes the news is entirely a journalistic decision. Organizational constraints within newsrooms matter, but the institutional contexts in which academics function also exert a force on source selection. Journalists may return to the same sources over and over again (as this Element suggests),

---

[54] This may be especially beneficial if media offices depend on researchers contacting them about new projects and publications as there may be systematic differences in which types of researchers are most likely to contact media offices.

[55] In the survey, 49.27% said that media requests are not part of their annual evaluations and 16.4% did not know whether media requests were part of the annual evaluation. However, in a different question, only 1.5% reported that their university actively discouraged speaking with the media.

but academics too have sticky networks. Media offices are more likely to turn to the same researchers when looking for new research (e.g., Marcinkowski et al., 2014); when asked "Is there anyone else I can speak to about this?" by journalists, academics likely turn to people in their own close networks.

The challenges inherent in sourcing, then, speak to larger puzzles: How do we break through the "stickiness" of networks? How do we create institutions that give people opportunities to share expertise – and be supported when doing so? Expert sources, then, are merely observable implications of these questions. If the news makes up the pictures of people in our heads, understanding the construction of political expertise helps us to better understand the costs of reflecting expert similitude.

References

Albæk, E. (2011). The interaction between experts and journalists in news journalism. *Journalism, 12*(3), 335–348. https://doi.org/10.1177/1464884910392851.

Allsop, J. (2022). The *Times*, Haiti, and the treacherous bridge linking history and journalism. *Columbia Journalism Review*.

Alter, K., Clipperton, J., Schraudenbach, E., & Rozier, L. (2020). Gender and status in American political science: Who determines whether a scholar is noteworthy? *Perspectives on Politics, 18*(4), 1048–1067.

Armstrong, C. L. (2004). The influence of reporter gender on source selection in newspaper stories. *Journalism & Mass Communication Quarterly, 81*(1), 139–154. https://doi.org/10.1177/107769900408100110.

Autzen, C. (2014). Press releases – the new trend in science communication. *Journal of Science Communication, 13*(3), C02.

Bansak, K., Hainmueller, J., Hopkins, D. J., & Yamamoto, T. (2021). Conjoint survey experiments. In J. N. Druckman & D. P. Green (eds.), *Advances in experimental political science* (pp. 19–41). Cambridge University Press.

Barnoy, A., & Reich, Z. (2020). Trusting others: A Pareto distribution of source and message credibility among news reporters. *Communication Research, 49*(2): 196–220. https://doi.org/10.1177/0093650220911814.

Baumgartner, F. R., & Jones, B. D. (2009). *Agendas and instability in American politics*. University of Chicago Press.

Berkowitz, D., & Beach, D. W. (1993). News sources and news context: The effect of routine news, conflict and proximity. *Journalism Quarterly, 70*(1), 4–12. https://doi.org/10.1177/107769909307000102.

Berlo, D. K., Lemert, J. B., & Mertz, R. J. (1969). Dimensions for evaluating the acceptability of message sources. *Public Opinion Quarterly, 33*(4), 563–576. https://doi.org/10.1086/267745.

Bisbee, J., Larson, J., & Munger, K. (2020). # polisci Twitter: A descriptive analysis of how political scientists use Twitter in 2019. *Perspectives on Politics, 20*(3): 879–900.

Blumell, L. E. (2017). She persisted ... and so did he. *Journalism Studies, 20*(2), 267–286. https://doi.org/10.1080/1461670x.2017.1360150.

Bourdieu, P. (2001). Television. *European Review, 9*(3), 245–256. https://doi.org/10.1017/s1062798701000230.

Boyce, T. (2006). Journalism and expertise. *Journalism Studies, 7*(6), 889–906. https://doi.org/10.1080/14616700600980652.

Boydstun, A. (2013). *Making the news: Politics, the media, and agenda setting.* University of Chicago Press.

Brown, D. K. (2020). Impressions of progress: How managers and journalists see DEI efforts. *Columbia Journalism Review.* //www.cjr.org/analysis/diversity-equity-inclusion-progress-newsrooms.php.

Brown, J. D., Bybee, C. R., Wearden, S. T., & Straughan, D. M. (1987). Invisible power: Newspaper news sources and the limits of diversity. *Journalism Quarterly, 64*(1), 45–54. https://doi.org/10.1177/107769908706400106.

Cann, D. J., & Mohr, P. B. (2001). Journalist and source gender in Australian television news. *Journal of Broadcasting & Electronic Media, 45*(1), 162–174.

Carlson, M. (2009). Dueling, dancing, or dominating? Journalists and their sources. *Sociology Compass, 3*(4), 526–542. https://doi.org/10.1111/j.1751-9020.2009.00219.x.

Coddington, M., & Molyneux, L. (2021). Making sources visible: Representation of evidence in news texts, 2007–2019. *Journalism Practice,* 1–19. https://doi.org/10.1080/17512786.2021.1949629.

Coleman, R. (2011). Journalists' moral judgement about children. *Journalism Practice, 5*(3), 257–271.

Comfort, S. E., Gruszczynski, M., & Browning, N. (2022). Building the science news agenda: The permeability of science journalism to public relations. *Journalism & Mass Communication Quarterly.*

Conway, B. A. (2021). "Sources and journalists" revisited: Proposing an interdependent approach to source use. *Journalism Practice, 16*(8): 1614–1634.

Cook, T. E. (2005). *Governing with the news: The news media as a political institution* (2nd ed.). University of Chicago Press.

Day, A. G., & Golan, G. (2005). Source and content diversity in op-ed pages: Assessing editorial strategies in the *New York Times* and the *Washington Post. Journalism Studies, 6*(1), 61–71. https://doi.org/10.1080/1461670052000328212.

Diekerhof, E. (2021). Changing journalistic information-gathering practices? Reliability in everyday information gathering in high-speed newsrooms. *Journalism Practice,* 1–18. https://doi.org/10.1080/17512786.2021.1922300.

Djerf-Pierre, M. (2007). The gender of journalism: The structure and logic of the field in the twentieth century. *Nordicom Review. 28,* 81–104. www.researchgate.net/profile/Monika-Djerf-Pierre/publication/273054543_The_gender_of_journalism_the_structure_and_logic_of_the_ field_in_the_twentieth_century/links/54f59f510cf2f28c1365c599/The-gender-of-journalism-the-structure-and-logic-of-the-field-in-the-twentieth-century.pdf.

Dudo, A., & Besley, J. C. (2016). Scientists' prioritization of communication objectives for public engagement. *PLOS One*, *11*(2), e0148867.

Dunaway, J. (2013). Media ownership and story tone in campaign news. *American Politics Research*, *41*(1), 24–53.

Eagly, A. H., & Karau, S. J. (2002). Role congruity theory of prejudice toward female leaders. *Psychological Review*, *109*(3), 573–598. https://doi.org/10.1037/0033-295x.109.3.573.

Esterling, K. (2009). *The political economy of expertise: Information and efficiency in American national politics*. University of Michigan Press.

Ferré, J. P. (1996). Review: Jack Fuller, *News values: Ideas for an information age*. *American Journalism*, *13*(3), 372–373. https://doi.org/10.1080/08821127.1996.10731847.

Freelon, D., Lopez, L., Clark, M. D., & Jackson, S. J. (2018). How Black Twitter and other social media communities interact with mainstream news. *Knight Foundation Report*. https://repository.upenn.edu/cgi/viewcontent.cgi?article=1802&context=asc_papers.

Galtung, J. (1995). Prospects for media monitoring: Much overdue, but never too late! *Javnost – The Public*, *2*(4), 99–105. https://doi.org/10.1080/13183222.1995.11008611.

Galtung, J., & Ruge, M. H. (1965). The structure of foreign news. *Journal of Peace Research*, *2*(1), 64–90. https://doi.org/10.1177/002234336500200104.

Gandy, O. H. (1982). *Beyond agenda setting: Information subsidies and public policy*. Ablex.

Gans, H. J. (1979). *Deciding what's news: A study of CBS Evening News, NBC Nightly News, Newsweek, and Time*. Pantheon Books.

Geertsema-Sligh, M., Bachmann, I., & Moody-Ramirez, M. (2020). Educating journalism students on gender and inequality. *Journalism & Mass Communication Educator*, *75*(1), 69–74.

Hanusch, F., & Nölleke, D. (2019). Journalistic homophily on social media. *Digital Journalism*, *7*(1), 22–44.

Harcup, T., & Deirdre, O. (2016). What is news? *Journalism Studies*, *18*(12), 1470–1488. https://doi.org/10.1080/1461670x.2016.1150193.

Horiuchi, Y., Markovich, Z., & Yamamoto, T. (2020). Measuring subgroup preferences in conjoint experiments. *Political Analysis*, *26*(2), 207–221.

Horiuchi, Y., Markovich, Z., & Yamamoto, T. (2021). Does conjoint analysis mitigate social desirability bias? *Political Analysis*, *30*, 535–549.

Imai, K., & Khanna, K. (2016). Improving ecological inference by predicting individual ethnicity from voter registration record. *Political Analysis*, *24*(2), 263–272.

Jia, S., Lansdall-Welfare, T., Sudhahar, S., Carter, C., & Cristianini, N. (2016). Women are seen more than heard in online newspapers. *PLOS One*, *11*(2), e0148434. https://doi.org/10.1371/journal.pone.0148434.

Johnson, M., Steve, S. P., & Aelst, P. V. (2018). Much ado about nothing? The low importance of Twitter as a sourcing tool for economic journalists. *Digital Journalism*, *6*(7), 869–888.

Jörgen, W., & Folke, J. (1994). Foreign news: News values and ideologies. *European Journal of Communication*, *9*(1), 71–89. https://doi.org/10.1177/0267323194009001004.

Kamau, C. (2019). Five ways media training helped me to boost the impact of my research. *Nature*, *567*, 425–426.

Kingdon, J. W. (1984). *Agendas, alternatives, and public policies*. Little, Brown.

Krupnikov, Y., Piston, S., & Bauer, N. (2016). Saving face: Identifying voter responses to black candidates and female candidates. *Political Psychology*, *37*(2), 253–273.

Krupnikov, Y., & Ryan, J. B. (2022). *The other divide*. Cambridge University Press.

Kruvand, M. (2012). "Dr. Soundbite": The making of an expert source in science and medical stories. *Science Communication*, *34*(5), 566–591. https://doi.org/10.1177/1075547011434991.

LaFrance, A. (2013). I analyzed a year of my reporting for gender bias and this is what I found. *Lady Bits on Medium*. https://medium.com/ladybits-on-medium/i-analyzed-a-year-of-my-reporting-for-gender-bias-and-this-is-what-i-found-a16c31e1cdf.

LaFrance, A. (2016). I analyzed a year of my reporting for gender bias (again). *The Atlantic*. www.theatlantic.com/technology/archive/2016/02/gender-diversity-journalism/463023/.

Leonhardt, D. (2018). I'm not quoting enough women. *New York Times*, MAY 13, 2018. https://www.nytimes.com/2018/05/13/opinion/women-sexism-journalism-conferences.html.

Lewis, J., Williams, A., & Franklin, B. (2008). Four rumours and an explanation. *Journalism Practice*, *2*(1), 27–45. https://doi.org/10.1080/17512780701768493.

Lippmann, W. (1922). *Public Opinion*. New York: Harcourt, Brace and Company.

Lupia, A. (2000). Evaluating political science research: Information for buyers and sellers. *PS: Political Science & Politics, 33*(1), 7–14.

Macharia, S., Wiley Blackwell, Karen Ross, Cosimo Marco Scarcelli, Ingrid Bachmann, Sujata Moorti, Valentina Cardo (2020). Global Media Monitoring Project (GMMP). In *The international encyclopedia of gender, media, and communication.* https://doi.org/10.1002/9781119429128.iegmc074.

Marcinkowski, F., Kohring, M., Fürst, S., & Friedrichsmeier, A. (2014). Organizational influence on scientists' efforts to go public: An empirical investigation. *Science Communication, 36*(1), 56–80.

McGregor, S. C. (2019). Social media as public opinion: How journalists use social media to represent public opinion. *Journalism, 20*(8), 1070–1086. https://doi.org/10.1177/1464884919845458.

McGregor, S. C., Searles, K., Maki, J., & Bhargava, R. (n.d.). Legitimating expertise: Expert source representation in the news. Paper presented at the annual meeting of the American Political Science Association.

McGuire, D. (2018). Historians are a great resource: Journalists, be sure to give them credit. *Columbia Journalism Review.*

McShane, S. L. (1995). Occupational, gender, and geographic representation of information sources in U.S. and Canadian business magazines. *Journalism & Mass Communication Quarterly, 72*(1), 190–204. https://doi.org/10.1177/107769909507200116.

Mellado, C., & Scherman, A. (2021). Mapping source diversity across Chilean news platforms and mediums. *Journalism Practice, 15*(7), 974–993.

Merkley, E. (2020). Are experts (news)worthy? Balance, conflict, and mass media coverage of expert consensus. *Political Communication, 37*(4), 530–549. https://doi.org/10.1080/10584609.2020.1713269.

Mitchelstein, E., Andelsman, V., & Boczkowski, P. J. (2019). Joanne Public vs. Joe Public: News sourcing and gender imbalance on Argentine digital media. *Digital Journalism, 7*(10), 1311–1327.

Molyneux, L., & Zamith, R. (2020). Surveying journalists in the "new normal": Considerations and recommendations. *Journalism, 23*, 153–170. https://doi.org/10.1177/1464884920935277.

Ossa, L. M. (2022). The mainstream media is getting academia wrong, still. *Esquire.* www.esquire.com/news-politics/a39038497/college-elitism-media-coverage-essay/.

Paul, N., Sui, M., & Searles, K. (2021). Look who's writing: How gender affects news credibility and perceptions of news relevance. *Journalism & Mass Communication Quarterly, 99*, 183–212. https://doi.org/10.1177/10776990211042595.

Peress, M. (2019). Measuring the research productivity of political science departments using Google Scholar. *PS: Political Science & Politics*, *52*(2), 312–317.

Petrovčič, A., Petrič, G., & Manfreda, K. L. (2016). The effect of email invitation elements on response rate in a web survey within an online community. *Computers in Human Behavior*, *56*, 320–329.

Porter, C., Méheut, C., Apuzzo, M., & Gebrekidan, S. (2022a). The root of Haiti's misery: Reparations to enslavers. *New York Times*.

Porter, C., Méheut, C., Gebrekidan, S., & Apuzzo, M. (2022b). The ransom: A look under the hood. *New York Times*.

Posetti, J., & Shabbir, N. (2022). The chilling: What more can news organisations do to combat gendered online violence? *ICJF*. www.icfj.org/sites/default/files/2022-05/UNESCO_GlobalStudy_chapt.3-whatmore_V4.pdf.

Posetti, J., Shabbir, N., Maynard, D., Bontcheva, K., & Abouelez, N. (2021). The chilling: Global trends in online violence against women journalists. *UNESCO*. https://en.unesco.org/sites/default/files/the-chilling.pdf.

Powers, A., & Fico, F. (1994). Influences on use of sources at large U.S. newspapers. *Newspaper Research Journal*, *15*(4), 87–97. https://doi.org/10.1177/073953299401500410.

Rattan, A., Chilazi, S., Georgeac, O., & Bohnet, I. (2019). Tackling the underrepresentation of women in media. *Harvard Business Review*. https://hbr.org/2019/06/tackling-the-underrepresentation-of-women-in-media.

Reese, S. D., & Shoemaker, P. J. (2016). A media sociology for the networked public sphere: The hierarchy of influences model. *Mass Communication and Society*, *19*(4), 389–410.

Reich, Z. (2011). Comparing reporters' work across print, radio, and online: Converged origination, diverged packaging. *Journalism & Mass Communication Quarterly*, *88*(2), 285–300.

Reid, R. (2021). Retaining women faculty: The problem of invisible labor. *PS: Political Science & Politics*, *54*(3), 504–506.

Rodgers, S., Thorson, E., & Antecol, M. (2000). "Reality" in the St. Louis post-dispatch. *Newspaper Research Journal*, *21*, 51–68.

Ross, K. (2007). The journalist, the housewife, the citizen and the press. *Journalism*, *8*(4), 449–473. https://doi.org/10.1177/1464884907078659.

Ross, K., Boyle, K., Carter, C., & Ging, D. (2016). Women, men and news. *Journalism Studies*, *19*(6), 824–845. https://doi.org/10.1080/1461670x.2016.1222884.

Rowe, D., & Brass, K. (2008). The uses of academic knowledge: The university in the media. *Media, Culture & Society, 30*(5), 677-698.

Schlesinger, P. (1990). *Rethinking the sociology of journalism: Source strategies and the limits of media-centrism.* Sage.

Shafer, J. (2022). Why historians are at war with the *New York Times. Politico.* https://www.politico.com/news/magazine/2022/05/23/new-york-times-historian-haiti-authoritative-source-00034511

Shoemaker, P. J., & Reese, S. D. (1996). *Mediating the message: Theories of influences on mass media content.* Longman.

Shoemaker, P. J., & Reese, S. D. (2014). *Mediating the message in the 21st century: A media sociology.* Routledge.

Shor, E., van de Rijt, A., Alex, M., Kulkarni, V., & Skiena, S. (2015). A paper ceiling. *American Sociological Review, 80*(5), 960–984. https://doi.org/10.1177/0003122415596999.

Sigel, L. V. (1973). *Reporters and officials.* Lexington Books.

Soley, L. C. (1992). *The news shapers: Sources who explain the news.* Praeger.

Steele, J. E. (1995). Experts and the operational bias of television news: The case of the Persian Gulf War. *Journalism & Mass Communication Quarterly, 72*(4), 799–812. https://doi.org/10.1177/107769909507200404.

Steiner, J. (2012). *The foundations of deliberative democracy: Empirical research and normative implications.* Cambridge University Press.

Stempel, G. H., & Culbertson, H. M. (1984). The prominence and dominance of news sources in newspaper medical coverage. *Journalism Quarterly, 61*(3), 671–676. https://doi.org/10.1177/107769908406100329.

Teele, D. L., & Thelen, K. (2017). Gender in the journals: Publication patterns in political science. *PS: Political Science & Politics, 50*(2), 433–447.

Tuchman, G. (1972). Objectivity as strategic ritual: An examination of newsmen's notions of objectivity. *American Journal of Sociology, 77*(4), 660–679. https://doi.org/10.1086/225193.

Tuchman, G. (1978). Professionalism as an agent of legitimation. *Communication, 28*(2), 106–113.

Venger, O. (2019). The use of experts in journalistic accounts of media events: A comparative study of the 2005 London bombings in British, American, and Russian newspapers. *Journalism, 20*(10), 1343–1359. https://doi.org/10.1177/1464884919830479.

Vogels, E. (2021). The state of online harassment. *Pew Research Center.* www.pewresearch.org/internet/2021/01/13/the-state-of-online-harassment/.

Wagner, A. (2020). Tolerating the trolls? Gendered perceptions of online harassment of politicians in Canada. *Feminist Media Studies*, 1–16. https://doi.org/10.1080/14680777.2020.1749691.

Wais, K. (2015). Genderizer: Gender prediction based on first names. *R package version 1.2.0.*

Weaver, D. H., Beam, R. A., Brownlee, B. J., Voakes, P. S., & Wilhoit, G. C. (2009). *The American journalist in the 21st century*. Routledge. https://doi.org/10.4324/9781410614568.

Willnat, L., Weaver, D. H., & Wilhoit, G. C. (2017). *The American journalist in the digital age: A half-century perspective*. Peter Lang Publishing.

Yong, E. (2018). I spent two years trying to fix the gender imbalance in my stories. *The Atlantic.*

Zeldes, G. A., & Fico, F. (2005). Race and gender: An analysis of sources and reporters in the networks' coverage of the 2000 presidential campaign. *Mass Communication & Society*, *8*(4), 373–385.

Zoch, L. M., & Turk, J. V. (1998). Women making news: Gender as a variable in source selection and use. *Journalism & Mass Communication Quarterly*, *75*(4), 762–775. https://doi.org/10.1177/107769909807500410.

Acknowledgements

We first and foremost would like to thank both the journalists and experts that inspired this project; your voices matter, and we thank you for your work. This project was supported by The Democracy Fund, the University of Arizona Commission on the Status of Women, The Reilly Center, and the Darlene and Thomas O. Ryder Professorship (held by Searles) both housed in the Manship School of Mass Communication at Louisiana State University. We'd like to thank Angelica Das and Jessica Mahone, without whom this project would not be possible. We also extend immense gratitude to our editor, Stuart Soroka, and the anonymous reviewers that improved this manuscript. Special thanks go to the friends and colleagues that offered feedback or assistance including: Shannon McGregor, Logan Molyneaux, Talia Stroud, Jenn Merolla, Benjamin Toff, Michael Wagner, Samara Klar, Jennifer Jerit, Nikki Usher, Aviv Barnoy, Kimberly Gross, James Robinson, David Broockman, Sonya Dal Cin, Christopher Drew, Ruth Moon, Leonard Apcar, Joshua Grimm, and Jerry Ceppos. Additional thanks go to the Louisiana State University Media Effects Lab for use of facilities and for access to the student subject pool. Thanks to Harry Applestein, Keegan Coon, Jacob Buckley, Jessica Maki, Maggie McDonnell, Caley Hewitt, Erica Russell, Simeon Burns, Sonia Yanovsky, Patrick Rose, and Cana Kim for their research assistance.

Cambridge Elements ≡

Politics and Communication

Stuart Soroka
University of California, Los Angeles

Stuart Soroka is a Professor in the Department of Communication at the University of California, Los Angeles, and Adjunct Research Professor at the Center for Political Studies at the Institute for Social Research, University of Michigan. His research focuses on political communication, political psychology, and the relationships between public policy, public opinion, and mass media. His books with Cambridge University Press include The Increasing Viability of Good News (2021, with Yanna Krupnikov), Negativity in Democratic Politics (2014), Information and Democracy (forthcoming, with Christopher Wlezien) and Degrees of Democracy (2010, with Christopher Wlezien).

About the Series

Cambridge Elements in Politics and Communication publishes research focused on the intersection of media, technology, and politics. The series emphasizes forward-looking reviews of the field, path-breaking theoretical and methodological innovations, and the timely application of social-scientific theory and methods to current developments in politics and communication around the world.

Cambridge Elements ≡

Politics and Communication

Elements in the Series

Home Style Opinion
Joshua P. Darr, Matthew P. Hitt, Johanna L. Dunaway

Power in Ideas
Kirsten Adams, Daniel Kreiss

Economic News
Rens Vliegenthart, Alyt Damstra, Mark Boukes, Jeroen Jonkman

The Increasing Viability of Good News
Stuart Soroka, Yanna Krupnikov

The Digital Public Arena
Andreas Jungherr, Ralph Schroeder

The Erosion of Civil Society in a Shifting Communication Ecology: Wisconsin and the Rise of U.S. Populism
Lewis A. Friedland, Dhavan V. Shah, Michael W. Wagner, Katherine J. Cramer, Chris Wells

Constructing Political Expertise in the News
Kathleen Searles, Yanna Krupnikov, John Barry Ryan and Hillary Style

A full series listing is available at: www.cambridge.org/EPCM

Printed in the United States
by Baker & Taylor Publisher Services